Helion & Company Limited
Unit 8 Amherst Business Centre
Budbrooke Road
Warwick
CV34 5WE
England
Tel. 01926 499 619
Email: info@helion.co.uk
Website: www.helion.co.uk
Twitter: @helionbooks
Visit our blog http://blog.helion.co.uk/

Designed and typeset by Farr out
    Publications, Wokingham, Berkshire
Cover design by Paul Hewitt, Battlefield
    Design (www.battlefield-design.co.uk)

ISBN 978-1-912390-19-9

British Library Cataloguing-in-Publication
    Data
A catalogue record for this book is available
    from the British Library

We always welcome receiving book
proposals from prospective authors.

CONTENTS

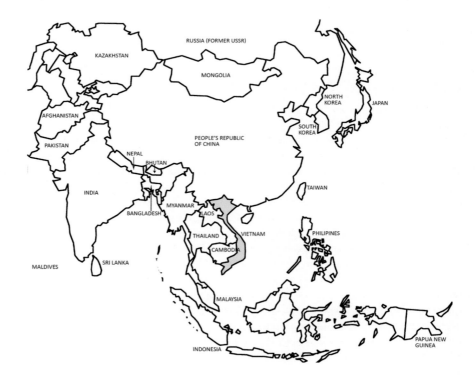

Note: In order to simplify the use of this book, all names, locations and geographic designations are as provided in *The Times World Atlas*, or other traditionally accepted major sources of reference, as of the time of described events.

ACKNOWLEDGEMENTS

The author wishes to express his special gratitude to all those individuals who contributed to this book. Specifically, I wish to express my deepest appreciation to Anthony J. Tambini, Cao Tan Loc, Chau Huu Loc, Dang Huy Lang, Do Khac Mai, Ha Minh Tay, Ho Dac Du, Ha Mai Viet, Huynh Sanh Thong, Huynh Ba Phuc, Huynh Thu Thoai, Jean Dunoyer, Ken Conboy, Le Quang Thuan, Le Xuan Lan, Mai Van Hai, Marc Koelich, Nguyen Tien Van, Nguyen Xuan Giac, Pham Long Suu, Pham Quang Khiem, Robert C. Mikesk, Roger Routin, Stephane Legoff, Ted Koppel, Terry Love, Timothy Keer, Timothy Pham, Tran Tan Tiep, Ung Buu Hoang Nguyen, Vo Ngoc Cac, and Vu Dinh.

All of them have provided extensive aid throughout the years in one or another form of related research and eventually made this book possible. He also wishes to present his deepest appreciation to Duncan Rogers and Tom Cooper of Helion & Company Publishing for their patience in the numerous delays in finalising this series about the fall of South Vietnam due to author's family problems arising these last two years.

ABBREVIATIONS

AA	anti-aircraft		**FSB**	Fire Support Base
AAA	anti-aircraft artillery		**PAVN**	People's Army of Vietnam (North Vietnamese Army)
ACS	Armoured Cavalry Squadron		**RF/PF**	Regional Forces/People's Forces (ARVN)
AFB	Air Force Base		**SAC**	Strategic Army Corps
APC	Armoured Personnel Carrier		**SAM**	Surface-to-air missile
ARVN	Army of the Republic of Vietnam (South Vietnamese Army)		**SP**	Self-propelled (artillery)
CO	Commanding Officer		**USAF**	United States Air Force
DMZ	Demilitarized Zone (separating North and South Vietnam)		**VNAF**	Vietnamese Air Force (Air Force of South Vietnam)
			VNN	Vietnamese Navy (Navy of South Vietnam)
FAC	Forward Air Controller (usually airborne controller in observation aircraft)		**VNMC**	Vietnamese Marine Corps

INTRODUCTION

On 27 January 1973 a peace accord that officially put an end to a conflict that had started 27 years previously was signed at Paris by the Secretary of State Henry Kissinger and the North Vietnamese representative Le Duc Tho. In exchange for the return of US prisoners of war, the United States withdrew its last forces while the North Vietnamese would be allowed to maintain their forces in the areas they controlled in South Vietnam. The different South Vietnamese "parties", i.e. the Saigon government and the Viet Cong, represented by the Provisional Revolutionary Government (PRG), would content themselves to sort out of their problems by the means of local elections to be organised by a National Reconciliation and Concord Committee. However, as it required unanimity on any decisions that formula could only led to paralysis. Then, it was not surprising that war resumed as both Hanoi and Saigon did not feel compelled by the agreement. Hanoi in fact now celebrated the event as a decisive step in its long process for reunification of the country with the withdrawal of the last American forces. Whether by a political process, through a provisional coalition government, or a military takeover, the North Vietnamese were ever determined to achieve their goal. President Nguyen Van Thieu of South Vietnam had been promised that Washington would continue to provide economic and military aid at the levels of the time of direct US involvement there. President Richard Nixon even told him that in the event of North Vietnamese "blatant violations" of the accord, he would "send back the B-52s". Thieu felt strong enough to confront the Communists and reject any suggestion of coalition with them as "a sure path to death" for him. At the ceasefire date, Army of the Republic of Vietnam (ARVN) troops controlled roughly 75 percent of the territory and most of the cities, representing 85 percent of the population. In the first year after the Paris Accord, the South Vietnamese managed to prevail over the North Vietnamese attacks, gradually escalating from local, to divisional, then army corps levels. Drastic cuts in American aid, starting in December 1973, reduced the South Vietnamese armed forces' budget from $2.1 billion to $700 million, and would have a dramatic effect on the military situation. By January 1975, it was estimated that there were enough supplies for only three months of high intensity fighting at the level of the Easter Offensive of 1972.

Hanoi closely followed the latest developments and finally decided to draw up plans for the final offensive to take over the South. The planned campaign was extended for two years, 1975–1976, as the ARVN's residual capabilities were still highly regarded. Furthermore, the North Vietnamese had to deal with their Soviet and Chinese allies which both favoured a status quo. The Chinese advised the North Vietnamese to devote all their efforts to rebuilding the North Vietnamese infrastructure after the devastating American air campaign of 1972 and to consolidate their economy. They also asked Hanoi to suspend any further military operation in the

The United States made a great effort to bolster the South Vietnamese armed forces before the implementation of the Paris Accords of January 1973 with Operation Enhance Plus. These M41 and M48 tanks had just been delivered to Saigon's New Port in December 1972. (US Army)

The drastic reduction in US aid as of December 1973 implied that even the one for one replacement of lost equipment, as agreed by the Paris Accords, would not be fulfilled. These M54 5-Ton trucks had just been delivered during Operation Enhance Plus. (US Army)

South for five years to enable a chance to implement the Paris Accords. Beijing in fact did not want a reunified Vietnam led by a communist regime that always expressed its independence from its more powerful northern neighbour and which showed more and more signs of alignment with Moscow. Furthermore, the Chinese did not want to antagonise Washington since both countries were

The ARVN's standard tank was the M41 Walker Bulldog. Initially conceived as a light reconnaissance tank, it was outgunned by North Vietnamese T-54s. (US Army)

The South Vietnamese requested more M48 Patton tanks to counter T-54s but only around 200 were delivered, equipping three squadrons and a mixed armoured battalion. These M48s of I Armoured Brigade were seen near a dump of vehicles wrecked in the fighting around Quang Tri. (US Army)

The US aid reduction greatly impaired ARVN mobility due to the rationing of fuel. This forced the South Vietnamese into a defensive posture and put an end to any corps-level offensive operations, like these M113 APCs of III Armoured Brigade seen during a foray into Cambodia in April 1974 to destroy PAVN rear bases. (US Army)

in a process of normalising their relations. The Soviets were also engaged in a détente policy with the United States and did not want to jeopardise the current negotiations on strategic arms limitations. Consequently, even though both Moscow and Beijing had reequipped the People's Army of Vietnam (PAVN) to make up the heavy losses suffered during the 1972 campaign, they withheld the delivery of artillery and tank ammunition to a bare minimum level. With only some 100,000 rounds of calibres up to 85mm available, the PAVN would not be able to carry out an all-out offensive. With all these factors taken into consideration, Senior General Vo Nguyen Giap, at the head of the Central Military Commission (CMC), had to carefully plan the coming campaign. He agreed with North Vietnam's Communist Party General Secretary Le Duan that it was now or never to grasp a "narrow window of opportunity" to win the war. That opportunity could be a political breakdown of the Saigon regime, like for example after a new coup d'état, or a decisive PAVN victory on a specific battlefield. Both the Politburo and General Headquarters would have to act fast before Washington could intervene. Le Duan also feared that both his Soviet and Chinese mentors would restrain him by imposing a last minute negotiated political settlement.

When Phuoc Binh, the capital of the Phuoc Long Province, was taken in January 1975 without American reaction, the North Vietnamese decided that it was now time to launch the new campaign. The ARVN was expecting an offensive against the northern part of the Central Highlands, closer to the North Vietnamese depots in Laos. However, thanks to a very efficient deception campaign, the PAVN

The ARVN's standard armoured reconnaissance vehicle was the Cadillac V100 Commando. It was operated by armoured cavalry units and by the mechanized platoons of the Regional Forces. (US Army)

By early 1975, efforts were also made to reduce the expenditure of artillery ammunition. Artillery units were now authorised to only engage clearly identified targets, while interdiction fire against suspected targets was denied. This ARVN M114 155mm howitzer was seen in the sector of Tay Ninh. (ARVN)

was able to move the equivalent of a whole army corps undetected to attack its southern part, quickly taking Ban Me Thout, the main city of the highlands. Suddenly, the North Vietnamese were well poised to strike north to destroy the remnants of the ARVN II Corps in their strongholds of Pleiku and Kontum, east towards the coast and then sever South Vietnam into two halves, or move south to join forces with the units deployed around Saigon for a decisive attack against the capital.

For weeks, his advisers suggested to President Thieu to shorten the front lines and to consolidate the dilapidated units into more defensive positions. But for political reasons, Thieu could not abide to the idea. He always requested that any positions should be defended at any costs and discarded any different strategy. But now, pressed by events, he decided upon a forceful redeployment of the South Vietnamese armed forces. On 11 March, in front of stunned high-ranking officers, he now ordered a wide range of strategic withdrawals and advocated the defence of only the most populous and economically significant parts of the country: the southern half or what was the old Cochinchina. Historically, a distinct "southern" identity had always existed there, and he planned to capitalise on this sentiment to turn the area into a last stronghold. In great secrecy, even the Americans were not informed, and in haste, he ordered the complete evacuation of the Central Highlands. The northern part of the country would also be sacrificed, and all the regular forces had to be pulled out into the Da Nang enclave. That

meant that no less than half of the country had to be abandoned to the enemy.

The withdrawal of the well-entrenched forces of Kontum and Pleiku along the disused Route 7B turned into a tragic rout. Without any meaningful preparations, the retreating column, joined by hundreds of thousands of civilians, was repeatedly attacked, trounced, and destroyed. On 3 April, the North Vietnamese not only occupied the whole Central Highlands but also the coastal plain between Quy Nhon and Cam Ranh Bay, with its huge military port developed at great expense by the Americans. If the collapse of the ARVN II Corps sent a shock wave throughout the country, the attempt to pull-out towards Da Nang would lead to another catastrophe of a greater magnitude and seal the fate of South Vietnam.

The ARVN also inherited a small number of former USAF XM706E2; a turretless version of the V100. (US Army)

By December 1974, the VNAF was forced to disband 10 of its squadrons due to budgetary cuts. This F-5A of the 536th Squadron, 63rd Wing at Bien Hoa, was parked in front of some mothballed Skyraiders of the 23rd Wing. However, due to the deteriorating situation, the latter were soon back in service. (Anthony Tambini)

VNAF C-130As suffered from structural damage to their wing spars and fuel tank leaks. A special program was initiated to send some airframes for general overhaul to Singapore by the end of 1974. An average of 14 Hercules was then available each day, out of a total of 32 delivered. (Pham Quang Khiem)

South Vietnamese President Nguyen Van Thieu visited a stand presenting captured PAVN equipment. It included 105mm and 122mm rocket launchers, AT-3 Sagger anti-tank missiles and SA-7 shoulder-launched man-portable missiles. The North Vietnamese suffered tremendous losses during the fighting of the Easter Offensive of 1972. (ARVN)

Both China and the Soviet Union reequipped the North Vietnamese after the Easter Offensive of 1972, in particular replacing lost tanks. By early 1975, the PAVN fielded a force of more than 700 tanks, mostly T-54s and Type 59s. (PAVN)

The North Vietnamese logistic system was tremendously developed, transporting some 843,106 tonnes of supplies from January 1974 to March 1975. That represented an increase of 1.6 times more tonnage delivered than the previous 13 years. A column of GAZ-63 trucks of Logistic Army 559 are seen here rolling down the Ho Chi Minh Trail. (PAVN)

North Vietnamese Communist Party General Secretary Le Duan, dressed in black, used all his influence in October 1974 to persuade the Politburo to launch the decisive and final campaign to conquer South Vietnam. A native from the South, he vowed to have occasion to return to his native land in his lifetime, and finally reunify the country. (PAVN)

The two main officers who planned the final campaign posed here together. On the left, Senior General Vo Nguyen Giap, the founder of PAVN and now Defence Minister and presiding over the Central Military Commission of the Politburo. Next to him, Senior General Van Tien Dung, the PAVN Commander in Chief who went south himself, in February 1975, to supervise the operations. (PAVN)

1

STRATEGIC MILITARY REGION I

The ARVN Military Region (MR) I was the most heavily defended of the country due to its proximity to the Demilitarized Zone (DMZ) that separated the two Vietnams. It was the scene of fierce fighting in 1972, and again in 1974, when the ARVN I Corps pushed back several coordinated, division-sized, North Vietnamese offensives. By 23 January 1973, when the Paris peace accord was supposed to be enforced, the South Vietnamese had not been able to reconquer all the lost territories. A task force advancing towards the DMZ was forced to pull back after experiencing heavy losses. Dong Ha, as well as the Cua Viet River estuary were firmly in North Vietnamese hands. In fact, the terrain clearly favoured the Communists. In addition to the whole area south of the DMZ, and which was turned into a huge storage area, heavily protected by anti-aircraft units, including batteries of S-75 (SA-2 'Guideline') SAMs, the North Vietnamese held all the plateaux and mountainous areas overlooking the narrow coastal plain. The Communist-controlled zones were directly linked to North Vietnam across the DMZ, as well as to their main logistic corridor, known as the Ho Chi Minh Trail, along the Laotian border.

The South Vietnamese held only the narrow coastal plain, between 15km to 30km wide at any point, with Hue, the ancient imperial capital, as well as Da Nang, the second largest city of the country. A major ridgeline that branches off the Annamite Mountain range and ends at the Hai Van Pass on the coast separated the two cities into discrete areas. The pass is the key terrain feature in I Corps. North of the pass are Quang Tri and Thua Thien provinces and the city of Hue, defended by South Vietnam's best three divisions: the 1st Division, and the national strategic reserve, the Marine and Airborne Divisions. Due to the importance of the area, the ARVN I Corps, under the command of Lieutenant General Ngo Quang Truong, probably one of the best South Vietnamese commanders, had set up a forward command post (I Corps Forward), under his very able deputy, Lieutenant General Lam Quang Thi. South of the pass is Quang Nam Province and Da Nang, with its strategic seaport and its huge air base, and defended by the ARVN 3rd Division. South of Da Nang, the South Vietnamese were stretched thin to defend a long area that included the coastal towns of Hoi An, Tam Ky, Chu Lai, and Quang Ngai. That sector was defended by the ARVN 2nd Division and two Ranger groups. In addition to his infantry and armour, Truong had the VNAF 1st Air Division, with 344 aircraft, including 72 A-37Bs (three squadrons), 20 F-5As (one squadron), and 16 brand-new F-5Es (one squadron). Detachments of eight to 10 F-5Es of Bien Hoa's 63rd Wing were also present on a rotational basis. There was also the Navy's 1st Coastal Zone, which included river craft, short range patrol vessels, and several deep-water ships.

The strategic ARVN I Corps, bordering North Vietnam, had been placed under the command of Lieutenant General Ngo Quan Truong since mid-1972. Considered as one the best South Vietnamese tacticians, but now placed under contradictory orders and deprived of his best troops – the Airborne and Marine Divisions – he could not uphold the coastal enclave concept and defend Da Nang. (ARVN)

The ARVN I Corps had experienced heavy fighting since the Easter Offensive of 1972, having occasion to capture many different items of North Vietnamese heavy equipment. Among them were this Chinese built Type 59 tracked artillery tractor, beside a T-54 and an M-46 130mm gun. (ARVN)

During the previous offensives the Communists were hampered by the lack of roads that had prevented the PAVN forces from building sufficient logistical stockpiles to maintain long offensives, while also providing ARVN units time to detect and react to their movements. Since the areas controlled by the South Vietnamese had better roads and shorter distances, the ARVN could shift reinforcements more quickly than the Communists. To mitigate that advantage, after the "ceasefire" the Communists had invested heavily in building an extensive road network in the area they had captured in 1972. Now, the PAVN could mass forces at multiple points in I Corps and could easily outflank the ARVN defensive positions.

Among the captured vehicles were these Chinese built K-63 APCs. (ARVN)

The North Vietnamese had also positioned the heaviest troop concentration in northern South Vietnam. PAVN had two major commands north of the Hai Van Pass; in the ARVN I Corps Forward area, they deployed the B4 Front and the 2nd Strategic Army Corps (SAC). The 2nd SAC was made up of the 304th, 324th, and 325th Divisions, the 673rd Anti-Aircraft Artillery Division, the 203rd Armoured Brigade, the 164th Artillery Brigade, the 219th Engineer Brigade, and the 463rd Signal Regiment. The B4 Front had the equivalent of

This PAVN 37mm anti-aircraft gun was captured in the area of Quang Tri. The gun would be towed back by an M113 APC. (ARVN)

a fourth infantry division, with three independent regiments, and eight local force Viet Cong battalions. South of the Hai Van Pass, the PAVN's B1 Front was made up the 2nd Division, in the southern Quang Nam Province, the 52nd Brigade in Quang Ngai Province, and almost a dozen independent Viet Cong battalions. The 52nd Brigade was a unique combined unit with three infantry battalions, two artillery battalions, one battalion of 37mm AA guns, and one sapper battalion. In addition, the B1 Front contained a division equivalent at Thuong Duc, in the form of two of 304th Division's regiments and one of 324th Division's regiments that had taken the town in August 1974. These forces were supported by the 574th Armoured Regiment, the 572nd and 576th Artillery Regiments, the 573rd Anti-Aircraft Artillery Regiment, the 83rd and 270th Engineer Regiment.

By weighing the two opposing forces, the ARVN seemed to have the upper edge. By taking into account the Regional and People Forces (RF/PF), General Truong had around 140,000 men under his command, supported by 418 guns and howitzers, and more than 500 armoured vehicles, including 449 tanks and APCs, as well as 64 M42 anti-aircraft tanks and V100 armoured cars. But many units of his regular troops were understrength due to heavy losses suffered in the previous year of heavy fighting. The RF/PFs, that represented more than half of the ARVN forces deployed in Military Region I, were for the most part mere militias that could not stand in the face of regular North Vietnamese units.

By comparison, and excluding the logistical and support troops manning the numerous logistical depots, the North Vietnamese deployed some 75,000 regular troops, supported by 358 artillery pieces, some 300 armoured vehicles, including 210 tanks and APCs, as well as 18 ZSU-57-2s, and 30 BTR-40 armoured reconnaissance cars. Unlike their enemy that was forced to disperse its forces to defend a wide range of urban centres, the North Vietnamese

An A-37B of the 61st Wing is pushed back inside its hardened shelter at Da Nang after a sortie. The attack wing had three squadrons of A-37Bs, and one each of F-5As and F-5Es. (VNAF)

North Vietnamese troops inspect a VNAF UH-1H that had been brought down. The widespread deployment of SA-7s by the North Vietnamese posed a new threat for VNAF aircraft operating at low level, especially slow movers like helicopters and FAC aircraft. (PAVN)

His G-2 Intelligence chief rightly predicted that I Corps would not be the main area targeted by the enemy for the coming dry season campaign; I Corps would be only a secondary theatre for Hanoi that would likely concentrate its forces in the northern Central Highlands. Attacks at first would be piecemeal in each province until all PAVN units were engaged by late April or early May 1975. The main targeted area would be around Quang Tri, where the North Vietnamese were the closest to their supply areas. Furthermore, the weather remained nasty, with an unusual extension of the rainy season up to February for that part of central Vietnam.

could quickly amass forces on a particular point of the front to achieve complete numerical superiority there and breach the South Vietnamese defensive lines for further exploitation.

Strategically, General Truong readied for two contingencies. In December 1974, the ARVN Joint General Staff (JGS) had predicted that Hanoi's main goal in I Corps' area for 1975 were to occupy the balance of Quang Tri Province and isolate Hue and Da Nang by cutting Route 1 at the Hai Van Pass. If the Communists attacked with the same force level as they had used in 1974, Truong believed he could defeat them. But if the North Vietnamese introduced into his Corps' area several strategic reserve divisions kept in North Vietnam, then he would be forced to retreat to a concentrated defence around Hue. If his central and southern fronts also collapsed, he would withdraw into enclaves centred on Da Nang and the Chu Lai peninsula in southern Quang Tin Province. Da Nang hosted several important military bases and depots while Chu Lai was the site of the ARVN 2nd Division's headquarters, with a large airfield and nearby port facilities.

In fact, Truong's predictions rather matched General Giap's own planning. The PAVN offensive in I Corps was only intended to tie down the two South Vietnamese strategic reserve divisions there, particularly the Airborne, so Saigon could not shift them to the Central Highlands. However, there were no detailed plans to attack the Airborne and Marine Divisions. Perhaps General Giap believed that if his forces threatened a vital target such as Hue, the ARVN would be forced to commit these two elite divisions. The PAVN would thereby succeed in tying down these units without incurring the risk of directly attacking them. However, if Giap did not believe his troops could liberate all of Quang Tri and Thua Thien provinces until 1976, he still hoped that by aggressively attacking, he might get a lucky break and capture a significant part of the lowlands.

Giap's plan also called for a major attack in Quang Tin Province. He sent his regulars against the RF, hoping for a quick victory to seize this vital area by early March 1975. The entire PAVN 2nd Division and the 52nd Brigade would shift from their normal operating areas in Quang Nam and Quang Ngai Provinces and converge on Tien Phuoc, with the goal of capturing Tam Ky. Quang Ngai local Viet Cong forces would launch supporting attacks to tie down the ARVN 2nd Division and prevent its reinforcing Quang Tin. In overall design, the North Vietnamese plan was a repeat of their 1974 plan, only with superior numbers attacking the same positions simultaneously instead of consecutively as they had done the previous year. The PAVN General Staff assumed direct control over the 2nd SAC and the B4 Front. Giap also assigned a new 2nd SAC commander, Major General Nguyen Huu An, who had just returned from a staff course in the Soviet Union. He was one of the PAVN's best commanders, having risen through the ranks from private to a major general. He was a regimental commander during the Dien Bien Phu battle, was the field commander during the famous Ia Drang battle at Landing Zones X-Ray and Albany in November 1965 against the US Army's 1st Cavalry Division, then commanded the PAVN 1st Division in Central Highlands. He later commanded forces in the Plain of Jars in Laos and fought during Operation Lam Son 719, the ARVN attempt to cut the Ho Chi Minh Trail in 1971. When the Easter Offensive bogged down in

A Marine of the VNMC in the area of Quang Tri displays a captured SA-7 launcher. (ARVN)

The northern sector of the ARVN I Corps was defended by the Marine Division. When ordered to pull back, the whole sector quickly crumbled. (ARVN)

1972, An was brought back to take over the 308th Division, leading it against the South Vietnamese counteroffensive in the Quang Tri area until the Paris Peace Agreement was signed.

In early February 1975, a group of senior 2nd SAC and B4 Front officers travelled to Hanoi to present their combined plan to attack northern Thua Thien. But Giap rejected it, considering that the Marine defences in that sector were simply too solid. A new plan called for the 2nd SAC to shift south and attack the hill country below Hue. The 324th Division would attack the same positions it had attacked the previous year, the Bong – Mo Tau area. There, the North Vietnamese would position their artillery on the captured hills to shell Route 1 and Hue's main airport, Phu Bai, effectively isolating ARVN I Corps Forward except by sea. The 325th Division would secretly depart the ceasefire line in Quang Tri and occupy the right flank of the 324th Division and would then attack the ARVN Fire Support Bases (FSB) positioned on the hills near the Truoi River, closer to the Hai Van Pass. The PAVN had been able to throw

the tactical situation off balance in ARVN I Corps Forward area by not relying on additional forces taken from the Central Reserve in North Vietnam but on drawing them from its own resources. While the B4 Front was to draw Truong's attention at the northern portion of Thuan Thien, the multi-division thrust south of Hue would be the primary sector for the entire campaign, with the 325th Division receiving orders to cut Route 1.

Within the nation-wide attack plan, and in support of the PAVN main thrust in the Central Highlands (see Target Saigon Volume 2), Giap imposed a tight timetable, with the opening first phase of the offensive against Hue to be started no later than 5 March. That first phase would be extended from March to early May, to be followed by phase two that would last from July to August. Giap ordered that no tanks or heavy long-range artillery – the dreaded D-74 122mm and M-46 130mm guns – were to participate in phase one. He needed to husband his remaining heavy weapons for the final attacks.

The Marines, with the RF troops, had built a series of strongpoints north of Quang Tri to hold off the North Vietnamese forces positioned at Dong Ha and along the DMZ. They were supported by the vehicles of I Armoured Brigade. (ARVN)

Marines patrolling the forwards positions ahead of Quang Tri. By early March 1975, they had pushed back the diversionary attacks carried out by the PAVN B4 Front. (ARVN)

of the US providing aerial imagery; the last American active program still current in Vietnam ended when a USAF RF-4C was shot down by the North Vietnamese during a reconnaissance mission in November 1974 near Dong Ha. The service had only a limited number of RF-5As that, as with the other attack aircraft, could not operate over the most-defended North Vietnamese-held areas due to a lack of any ECM equipment.

General Truong was fully aware that he had barely contained an attack by the PAVN 324th Division in the hill country in the summer of 1974. He was now very pessimistic about his chances to stop a new offensive by a reinforced enemy. His signals intelligence (SIGINT) alarmed him when it reported that it had detected signs of infiltration by the PAVN 316th and 341st Divisions of the Central Reserve. In fact, the former was still in North Vietnam, while the later had just been sent into the ARVN III Corps' area. The sophisticated North Vietnamese SIGINT deception plan here also succeeded exceedingly well in the Central Highlands sector. Nevertheless, Truong tried by any means possible to disrupt the PAVN build-up on his western flank by mobilising the scare VNAF resources.

Having just one month to meet the schedule, B4 Front's engineer units began to carve roads out of the rocky and hilly terrain to move vehicles and 85mm and 105mm artillery. At first, the local Routes 71 and 73 were repaired, then new lateral roads leading to the depots along the Ho Chi Minh Trail and in the A Shau Valley were built. Finally, 75km of side roads were built to several hills along both sides of the Truoi River. In all, the North Vietnamese had added nearly 400km of additional roads on the western perimeter of ARVN I Corps Forward since January.

The ARVN intelligence had only a murky view of the deployments in I Corps sector. The VNAF could not compensate for the cessation

The PAVN attacks in northern Quang Tri sector on 5 March were mostly pushed back by RF troops, supported by a mobile armoured task force. These two M41s of the 7th ACS were seen during a counterattack. (ARVN)

The real objective of the North Vietnamese opening campaign was the hilly country southwest of Hue. The South Vietnamese covered this sector with a series of Fire Support Bases where they positioned artillery. (ARVN)

The South Vietnamese mounted a series of air strikes against the newly discovered Ruong Ruong storage area, south of the A Shau Valley, with its truck and tank parks and a 150,000-gallon fuel tank farm in January 1975. Since the VNAF sorties faced ever-stronger enemy air defences, its aircraft began attacking parts of the enemy logistical build-up at night with the help of the AN/TBP-1A Beacon Only Bombing System (BOBS) guidance. The first missions were directed against the A Shau and Ben Vanh Valleys. The attacks were usually carried out from altitudes of between 10,000 and 15,000ft (3,048–4,572m), by formations of between 20 and 24 A-37Bs, which dropped their bombs simultaneously, upon command of the radar controller. Another major North Vietnamese concentration of troops was meanwhile detected at Thu Bon, west of Da Nang and subjected to the fiercest attack flown by the VNAF up to that

date: a formation of nine C-130A transports under BOBS guidance bombed the area, each simultaneously dropping a total of 32 Mk 32 500lb bombs, saturating the zone with no fewer than 288 bombs.

In addition to air attacks, the North Vietnamese engineers had to struggle with continuing rains that turned many of the newly opened roads into a quagmire and many artillery tractors were bogged down in the mud. The last leg to position artillery pieces into firing pits atop the hills was often the most difficult. For example, a group of 200 soldiers of the 84th Artillery Regiment of the 325th Division took a whole day to push and pull a 105mm howitzer through a muddy trail uphill. Despite all their efforts, Major General Nguyen Huu An realised that the engineering units could not finish their route-opening task in time. He dispatched his deputy, Major General Hoang Dan to Hanoi, to request an additional delay.

Many of the ARVN outposts on the line of crests west of Hue were only resupplied by helicopters. This UH-1H of the 51st Wing used as a tiny platform a landing spot. (ARVN)

Soldiers of the ARVN 1st Division take shelter facing enemy artillery while defending the hilltops southeast of Hue. (ARVN)

The North Vietnamese positioned this M-30 122mm howitzer to support an attack against Tien Phuoc by the PAVN 2nd Division. (PAVN)

The task of severing Route 1 south of Hue was assigned to the PAVN's 324th Division. Some trucks of the unit bogged down in soft soil and are seen here being pulled out by an AT-T artillery tractor. (PAVN)

To counter the North Vietnamese advance in the Tien Phuoc–Tan Ky sector, the 3rd Airborne Brigade was sent there to deal with the PAVN 2nd Division. It came along with a battery of M102 105mm howitzers. (PAVN)

Giap finally relented and agreed that the B4 Front would attack on schedule on 5 March in Quang Tri to draw the ARVN's attention. The 324th Division, as well as two B4 Front regiments, would assault Mo Tau and other nearby hills three days later. The 325th Division would start its offensive only on 27 March on the right flank of the 324th Division.

To draw ARVN attention northward, on 5 March the PAVN held a large-scale field exercise near Cua Viet to give the impression of an impending offensive. The B4 Front shifted troops and sent out tanks to drive through several areas. Fake radio messages were also sent, suggesting the deployment of the 308th Division of the Central Reserve to the area, though for the moment that unit was still in the Hanoi area. ARVN intelligence was confused but Lieutenant General Thi did not seem to take the bait. When the PAVN B4 Front

attacked the next day with five local forces battalions, the ARVN did not rush in additional forces. Thi left the first line defences as the responsibility of the Regional Forces and the Rangers, keeping the Marines in reserve to wait and see how the situation would develop. It soon turned out to be only a diversionary operation, and even though some Communist probes had breached the front lines they were pushed back in two days. At Hill 51, a VNMC battalion counterattacked and retook the lost position, helped by very efficient air support. Southeast of Hue, two Communist local force battalions penetrated behind ARVN lines and moved to the coast where they entrenched near the Faifoo Peninsula. General Thi immediately

The rest of the Airborne Division was still engaged in low-level fighting southwest of Hue against the depleted PAVN 304th Division. These wounded paratroopers awaited evacuation under the protection of an M48 tank. (ARVN)

reacted and directed a BOBS-guided dawn air strike by a group of 24 A-37Bs, dropping simultaneously their loads of CBU-24A/B cluster bombs. An ARVN armoured task force then moved in to overwhelm the last resistance.

These first North Vietnamese probes had nevertheless created panic among the civilians, and around 100,000 of them, roughly half of the population of the Quang Tri Province, fled towards Hue. When the local authorities struggled to accommodate all the refugees, the PAVN 2nd SAC finally entered into action, when the 324th Division attacked positions on Mo Tau Hill. On 8 March, two regiments of that unit struck ARVN outposts, while two B4 Front regiments attacked several other important hills. Mo Tau was overrun, but numerous air strikes, some coordinated personally by Lieutenant General Thi, enabled a counterattack to regain the hill. After two days of heavy fighting, the North Vietnamese could not advance much in the face of the stiff resistance of the ARVN 1st Division. Only a few small hills had been captured along with one major one, Hill 224, the gateway to the Bong Mountains. Hill 224 dominated the north side of the Truoi River and stands between Mo Tau and the Mom Kum Sac hills, which command the river's south side. When Hill 224 was overrun, the ARVN 1st Division led a counterattack that recaptured part of it. After four days of fighting, the South Vietnamese had driven back the PAVN 324th Division with heavy losses.

But the North Vietnamese were more successful in opening a new front at the ARVN's weakest point, the sector of Tien Phuoc, weakly defended by the ARVN 916th RF Battalion. The area was simultaneously assaulted on 10 March by the PAVN 2nd Division plus major elements of the 52nd Brigade from Quang Ngai Province under command of Major General Nguyen Chanh. The main thrust was carried out by the PAVN 31st Regiment, supported by a dozen

In addition to the paratroopers, the ARVN I Corps also dispatched the 12th Ranger Group and the armour of the 12th ACS to reinforce Tam Ky. (ARVN)

The whole defence concept of the ARVN I Corps was the quick displacements of armoured task forces along the coastal Route 1 to the threatened sectors. In the northern Hai Van Pass, a task force was made up of the 7th and 17th Armoured Cavalry Squadrons, and part of the 20th Tank Squadron. These M41s belonged to the 7th ACS. (ARVN)

An ARVN convoy of ammunition trucks, moving along Route 1 north of the Hai Van Pass, made up of M123 10-ton tractor trucks. (ARVN)

Each armoured task force was reinforced by a battalion of M107 175mm SP guns. (ARVN)

Escorting the military convoys along Route 1 was this M42 anti-aircraft artillery tank. (ARVN)

85mm, 105mm and 122mm guns and howitzers. The outgunned RF troops were forced to retreat towards Tam Ky and the town was taken after a fight of four hours. The next day, Brigadier General Tran Van Nhut, CO of the ARVN 2nd Division, hurried to Tam Ky to plan a relief operation to recapture Tien Phuoc. Truong also dispatched his reserve, the 12th Ranger Group and the M41s and M113s of the 12th ACS, to reinforce Tam Ky. However, when the 5th Regiment, 2nd Division, began its attack, radio intercept revealed the real size of the North Vietnamese forces in the area. They were just being reinforced by the 94th and 96th Regiments of B1 Front

in southern Quang Ngai. Truong then prudently ordered a halt to the operation. Bad news continued to arrive when the intelligence indicated that PAVN Quang Tri local forces had replaced the 325th Division along the northern ceasefire line. When prisoners from the 324th Division confirmed the arrival of the 325th Division in the hill country south of Hue, Truong immediately reacted. Tien Phuoc was no longer the priority. Truong immediately realised that the 325th Division's presence enabled the PAVN to strike in multiple directions to put additional pressure on his 1st Division, to seize the strategic Hai Van Pass, or to attack Da Nang from the north. On 10 March, while the PAVN 304th Division at Thuong Duc remained in its bunkers, he shifted one Airborne brigade to cover Da Nang's northern approaches. He also ordered the 14th Ranger Group to depart Quang Ngai Province and fly to Da Nang to reconstitute his reserve and moved a 3rd Division regiment to cover northern Quang Tin Province after the departure of the 12th Rangers.

In fact, the ARVN I Corps intelligence here had suffered a major breakdown, being unable to assess the exact status of the PAVN 304th Division. The unit was so badly battered from the previous year's battle at Thuong Duc that it was incapable of offensive operations.

Only the division's 9th Regiment, on its way from Quang Tri, was combat-ready. This failure to accurately gauge the 304th's status led Truong to tie down his best troops and affected his military decision-making. Truong then believed that he was forced to concentrate a sizeable blocking force west of Da Nang to protect the city.

2
THE PULL-OUT OF THE RED BERET ANGELS

Despite the loss of Tien Phuoc and a few positions south of Hue, after the first week of action Truong was confident that he had halted the North Vietnamese offensive. But amid this confidence, on 12 March, the JGS cabled Truong ordering him to release the Airborne Division for an immediate return to Saigon. With the ARVN's strategic reserves tied down in I Corps, the JGS needed the division to help retake Ban Me Thuot in the Central Highlands and defend Saigon. In fact, there was almost no second line of resistance around the capital.

The order came as a shock. With the 325th Division poised in the hills, and the 304th Division entrenched west of Da Nang, removing the paratroopers, popularly known as the "Red Beret Angels", would strip Truong's defences around South Vietnam's second largest city. He immediately requested and was granted an audience with President Thieu. Arriving in Saigon on 13 March, he passionately pleaded his case. Taking his best unit during an enemy offensive was folly. Without the Airborne Division, he would need to shift the Marine Division from Quang Tri to cover his lines west of Da Nang. The resultant transfer of forces to protect the city meant in

essence abandoning Quang Tri. Defending Hue would also prove problematic. Further, the loss of the Airborne would adversely affect military and civilian morale. The civilians were well aware that the Red Berets, who had already saved Da Nang the previous year, were essential to the region's defence. Pulling out the paratroopers would be interpreted as the government giving up I Corps. The population would subsequently flee, like in the Central Highlands, compounding Truong's already massive refugee problem. If Thieu's order stood, the sweeping changes it would entail threatened to destroy the I Corps.

But Thieu persisted and explained to Truong his new strategic concept. With the severe aid cuts, and no hope for the return of the US airpower to help to stem the North Vietnamese attacks, his best option was to consolidate his forces and try to survive a new dry season offensive. Afterwards, the ARVN would prepare for what he was sure would be a major North Vietnamese offensive in 1976. Turning to a map, he outlined for Truong his vision of the future of South Vietnam. Thus, he had made the decision to defend only those areas critical to the survival of the country. In I Corps, only

On 17 March, the first elements of the Airborne Division were pulling back from the I Corps. These paratroopers are boarding VNAF C-130As at Da Nang AB. (ARVN)

Da Nang and the surrounding areas were to be held at all costs. All other areas, including Hue, could be abandoned to enable the concentration of forces for the defence of the Da Nang enclave. Thieu informed Truong that his idea was to seek a "last enclave, a beachhead along the coast that would serve as a landing area if the Americans decided to return". Moreover, by concentrating the Marine Division, three infantry divisions, four regimental-sized Ranger groups, and an armoured brigade, Thieu hoped to lure the North Vietnamese into a set piece battle. The Marine and the 1st and 3rd Divisions would be deployed to defend Da Nang's outer perimeter defence line. The 2nd Division, the Rangers and the I Armoured Brigade would be the reserve force.

On paper, that seemed a very seductive idea but carrying out such redeployment in the middle of an enemy offensive on several fronts, while pulling out the elite paratroopers, would be a formidable undertaking. Thieu did not seemed to realise the difficulties of the task. The ongoing disaster in the Central Highlands "redeployment" should have rung alarms when the withdrawing columns were entangled by a mass of civilian refugees fleeing the arrival of the Communists. Truong reminded Thieu that many peoples in Da Nang and Hue were fearful of the Communists, having in mind the thousands of civilian executions taking place in Hue in 1968 during the weeks where the Viet Cong held parts of the city. During the Easter Offensive of 1972, columns of refugees along Route 1 were also mercilessly pounded by the North Vietnamese artillery. Truong, instead, pleaded for a contraction of his front lines and a gradual withdrawal towards a series of coastal enclaves. Thieu backed off and gave Truong more latitude and allowed him to pull back, in addition to Da Nang, towards Hue and Chu Lai. The defence of Hue was particularly important for Truong for its symbolic value, being the ancient imperial capital. Truong was also emotionally committed to the defence of the city, being personally involved in its reconquest in 1968 at the head of the 1st Division with the US Marines. The JGS however warned both Thieu and Truong that the now depleted Vietnamese Navy (VNN) would not have enough means to sustain simultaneously three coastal enclaves.

Whatever the obstacles to overcome, Truong was ordered to develop a plan for the necessary redeployments. He would receive the newly formed 468th Marine Brigade as a replacement for the Airborne Division, who would start moving by 17 March. Truong begged for more time to phase the withdrawal. Once the situation was stable, he could shift forces, but rapid changes would invite panic. Thieu instead offered a compromise. Truong could stagger the movement one Airborne brigade at a time, but the entire withdrawal was to be completed by the end of March. He also reminded him that he had already been instructed in December 1974 to be ready to send his paratroopers outside his command zone for the defence of more exposed areas within 72 hours and that he should have planned for such a contingency. But even though Truong knew in principle that this was a possibility, to have the withdrawal called for so hurriedly and in the middle of an enemy offensive was a severe blow.

When a sombre Truong returned to his headquarters in Da Nang, he did not inform his subordinates of the full scope of the discussions he had had with the President. In fact, Thieu had ordered him to keep secret the details of his national strategy of redeployment of forces. The fear of Communist spies and a collapse of civilian and military morale imposed a ban on any discussion of that decision. In reality, as the events would prove, that would only increase confusion, misunderstandings, rumours and plunge whole areas into chaos when the troops began to withdraw. On 14 March, he

Lieutenant General Ngo Quang Truong, first from right, went to Quang Tri to discuss with the CO of the Marine Division, Major General Bui The Lan, second from right, about the redeployment of his unit for the defence of Hue and Da Nang, replacing the departing Airborne Division. Second from left is the CO of the VNMC 258th Brigade, Colonel Ngo Van Dinh. (VNMC)

convened a meeting with his senior officers, but informed them only of the withdrawal of the Airborne Division. The defensive positions held by the unit would be taken over by the Marine Division that had to move out of its operational area north of the I Corps. None of his province chiefs, division, VNAF and VNN commanders were told of the enclaves strategy. If informed in time, they would surely have developed more elaborate plans. The only order given to them was to maintain their positions and to preserve their artillery ammunition for an expected wide-scale enemy offensive. Following the same logic, the VNAF 1st Air Division was also limited to around 40 strike sorties a day.

Truong ordered the 369th Marine Brigade to depart Quang Tri and replace the 3rd Airborne Brigade at Thuong Duc. Soon after, some of the paratroopers boarded VNAF C-130As for Saigon. Meanwhile the 14th Ranger Group moved up to Hai Lang District in Quang Tri Province to replace the departing 369th Marine Brigade. The 258th Marine Brigade and the Marine Division headquarters would follow and replaced the 2nd Airborne Brigade. That unit was moved down to Da Nang docks to be shipped to Saigon. The armoured task force attached to I Corps Forwards, made up of a troop of M48 tanks, the M41s and M113s of the 7th and 17th ACS and a battalion of M107 175mm SP guns, was regrouped at Thuan An port, on 18 March, waiting to be shipped to Da Nang. Lieutenant General Lam Quang Thi, CO of the I Corps Forward, deprived of its main striking force, did the utmost to secure Route 1 on the Hai Van Pass, as, if it was closed, he would not have the means to reopen it

The departing Marines north of Quang Tri were replaced by RF troops and the 14th Ranger Group, with the support of the armour of the 17th ACS. (ARVN)

and then would be isolated from the rest of the Corps. In return for the 369th Marine Brigade, Thi was given the 14th Ranger Group. He left the 147th Marine Brigade north of Hue. He also put the 258th Marine Brigade headquarters and one battalion on the Hue side of the Hai Van Pass, while another battalion remained near Hue. The third battalion went with the 369th Marine Brigade to Thuong Duc. Not until the 468th Marine Brigade arrived from Saigon on 21 March did he shift the 258th Marine Brigade headquarters into Quang Nam Province.

While the ARVN was reshuffling its forces around Hue, the PAVN 324th Division resumed its attacks around Hill 224. Over several days, control shifted back and forth. On 16 March, the South Vietnamese had recaptured the entire peak. Supply problems prevented the 324th Division from launching further attacks. Its commander pleaded for the support of the neighbouring 325th Division but the 2nd SAC commander, Major General Nguyen Huu An, ruled out that option. He strictly adhered to Giap's plan for continuing to forward deploy the 325th Division to its jump-off positions, to be ready to cut Route 1 later. Meanwhile, in Quang Ngai Province, low-level fighting continued, but neither side could make any headway. On 13 March, noticing the pull-out of the 14th Ranger Group and the 5th Regiment, local Communist forces pushed

forward. By 16 March they were pressing towards Quan Ngai City, forcing back a regiment of the 2nd Division. To shorten his lines, Truong ordered the abandonment of two western districts in Quang Ngai Province. He personally supervised the air evacuation of one Ranger battalion and numerous civilians. Over two days, some 2,500 civil servants and their families were rescued by helicopters.

But now, the most difficult task for the ARVN was pulling out the Marines along the Thac Han River in the northern part of the I Corps with the arrival of the 14th Ranger Group there on 16 March. The unit, badly understrength due to heavy attrition suffered during the fighting in 1974, with only 1,400 soldiers out of a full complement of 2,324 men, took over the defensive positions of the departing, 3,500-strong 369th Marine Brigade, on the western side of Route 1. The Rangers put one battalion on the river, and another facing the mountains and held one in reserve. The next day, the 258th Marine Brigade departed from the eastern side of Route 1, leaving only the Quang Tri RF group to continue defending the area. As already indicated, the last Marine brigade, the 147th, remained dug in northwest of Hue. Once again, as during the fighting in 1974, Thi had deliberately placed his weakest units on the ceasefire line, betting that the North Vietnamese would not cross it.

3
STRATEGIC OPPORTUNITY

Thi assumed that the PAVN would not cross the Thac Han River in force because that could be interpreted as a direct invasion from North Vietnam across the DMZ separating the two countries. Such a blatant violation of the "ceasefire" could possibly lead to a strong US reaction. Hanoi was now convinced that Washington would not intervene again and that if a long-sought opportunity appeared on the battlefield, like the collapse of a whole ARVN regional theatre of operations, Giap was ready and determined to fully exploit it. And Giap seemed to discern that opportunity when on 15 March PAVN intelligence reported that the 14th Ranger Group had shifted to Da Nang. Although he was then focused on the Central Highlands, upon studying the Rangers' movement, combined with the pull-out from Pleiku, he now discerned a pattern. He suspected the ARVN was retreating into the long-feared enclaves strategy. He immediately ordered attacks in I Corps to prevent an enclave from forming at Da Nang. On 17 March, he ordered Nhuyen Huu An to shift to the

Opportunity Plan: liberate Hue, the rest of Thua Thien, and Quang Tri. Giap told him to "step up your attacks from the west against the enemy's regular army units, cut off and strategically divide Hue from Da Nang."

On 18 March, Giap received more vital intelligence, indicating that the Airborne Division was withdrawing to Saigon. Noticing the very thin ARVN defence along the Thach Han River, Giap concluded that the South Vietnamese were abandoning Quang Tri Province. Giap immediately ordered the B4 Front to attack across the river: he had just called Lieutenant General Thi's bluff. Later that day, Giap received a second important message detailing the South Vietnamese strategic redeployments of forces in both I and II Corps areas. The Politburo and the Central Military Commission (CMC) were immediately convened to discuss the latest developments. Giap made a thorough presentation of the different theatres of operations in the South. He outlined his belief that ARVN was pulling back into enclaves and that it was crucial to push on hard now in order to prevent this. Strongly supported by the Party's General Secretary Le Duan, he recommended that all of the PAVN should be engaged now for the decisive campaign to liberate the South. Le Duan suggested that forces in the Central Highlands would join with those of the B2 Front for a direct attack against Saigon. However, more wisely, Giap indicated that if Saigon remained the ultimate prize, the first goal would be to destroy the South Vietnamese armed forces in I Corps and liberate Hue and Da Nang.

The Politburo resolution was now the liberation of South Vietnam in only one year, 1975, instead of two. Giap decided to engage the whole of the PAVN's remaining assets for the offensive. The strategic reserve retained in North Vietnam, the elite 1st SAC, made up of the 308th Division, the 312th Division, and the 320B Division, the 367th Anti-Aircraft Artillery Division, the 202nd Armoured Brigade, the 45th Artillery Brigade, the 299th Engineer Brigade, and the 204th Signal Regiment, was preparing to be sent South. All restrictions about the use of long-range artillery (D-74 122mm and M-46 130mm guns) and tanks were lifted. The 201st and 215th Armoured Brigades as well as the 207th Armoured Regiment, kept in reserve in the North, were also sent to the South. In fact, Giap decided to engage the whole North Vietnamese tank corps of around 700 tanks for the campaign.

What had been feared by Truong happened when the Marines pulled back along the Thach Han River line. Many civilians began to abandon their houses and tried to seek shelter at Hue or Da Nang. Soon, some 300,000 refugees settled in the streets of the ancient capital. That exodus would accelerate in the following days and contributed, like in the Central Highlands, to the disintegration of the whole ARVN I Corps. Rumours began to be spread that a new secret partition plan of the country had been arranged by the great powers and that President Thieu was being implemented it. That the area from the 17th Parallel down south to the 13th Parallel would

be handed over to the Provisional Revolutionary Government (Viet Cong), and that a new cycle of negotiations would be arranged with Hanoi.

The flow of refugees was such that it impeded any troop redeployments, with a choke point at the Hai Van Pass. General Truong ordered check points to be set up, but the traffic jam became worst. Fearing that the North Vietnamese artillery would open fire

The massive exodus of civilians fleeing towards Da Nang completely congested the Hai Van Pass, impending the movement of military units. (ARVN)

The departure of the Marines from Quang Tri created panic among the local civilians. Entire villages began to empty of their inhabitants who feared the Communists' arrival, and people moved south towards Hue and Da Nang. (VNN)

on the columns of civilian vehicles, like they did in 1972, Truong decided to reopen Route 1 to them. Eventually, more than 400,000 refugees settled into Da Nang, out of a city's population of 1,000,000 inhabitants. And that number was growing each day.

On 19 March, General Truong flew to Saigon again to brief President Thieu on the withdrawal plans he had developed. Truong offered two options: either a retreat north and south along Route 1 to Da Nang, or a pullback into enclaves centred on Hue, Chu Lai, and Quang Ngai City, and then a withdrawal by sea. Since refugees already jammed Route 1, the enclave – sea withdrawal was the better option. Truong recommended defending the enclaves as long

as possible, and then withdrawing to Da Nang when the pressure became too great. He would give up Chu Lai and Quang Ngai first, and only then Hue. Both ARVN Chief of Staff, General Cao Van Vien, and Thieu recommended a different plan. They wanted Truong to withdraw in successive phases towards Da Nang as Thieu believed that soon the enemy would exert maximum efforts to cut Route 1 at the Hai Van Pass. But finally, Thieu let Truong defend Hue but warned him that he would make a maximum effort to keep open Route 1 so that the 1st Division could safely withdraw to Da Nang. Thieu also promised to make a television and radio broadcast that night to reassure his people.

4

FALL OF HUE

When receiving the order to initiate phase two for the B4 Front sooner than expected, with the offensive scheduled for 21 March, Major General Nguyen Huu An fulminated about the previous restrictions on using heavy artillery and tanks. Most of these assets were still in their storage areas around Dong Ha, south of the DMZ or in the A Shau Valley. The 203rd Armoured Brigade had its four battalions arrayed between Dong Ha and the Laotian border. He argued that if the armour had been placed in jump-off attack positions beforehand, he could attack more forcefully and more decisively. But for the moment, only the 7th Company, 2nd Armoured Battalion, was near the Thach Han River line. Its dozen T-54s crossed the ARVN defensive line in the night of 19 March, spearheading a motorised task force made up with the local force 3rd Battalion mounted on trucks, and supported by a battery of ZIS-2 57mm anti-tank guns and another of D-44 85mm guns. They drove along the seashore before veering right towards the defensive positions held by an ARVN RF Group, around 10km behind the South Vietnamese lines. The appearance of the PAVN tanks caused panic among the South Vietnamese regional units that abandoned their positions. With their families and the Marines gone, and nothing but deserted villages all around them, they had little to fight for. The PAVN task force then drove for the district town of Hai

Lang, south of Quang Tri City, and held by elements of the 14th Ranger Group. After a brief fire fight, the Rangers pulled back.

Simultaneously, three other B4 Front battalions, the 8th, 812th and 20th, also crossed over the Thach Han River, while the 14th Battalion attacked from the west of Route 1. The B4 Front's assets were also reinforced by the independent 46th Regiment, just coming from North Vietnam. At 4:00 p.m., the Communists entered Quang Tri City without a fight. The fall of Quang Tri, a place that was the most contested area of the whole 1972 Easter Offensive, crushed South Vietnamese morale.

With his northern front lines crumbling, General Thi ordered the Rangers and what remained of the Quang Tri RF to retreat and take up defensive positions along the My Chanh River, establishing a new defensive belt north of Hue. He also ordered the 7th Marine Battalion, 258th Brigade, currently sitting at the port of Thuan An outside of Hue awaiting ships, to withdraw to Da Nang, to halt its redeployment.

Facing this disastrous development, Truong called the President. He recommended that Thieu hold off on his speech about defending Hue until he could better understand the situation. Truong further asked to retain the last Airborne brigade until 31 March. This would give the population some confidence that the government intended

On 19 March, the PAVN B4 Front's forces crossed the Thach Han River when the South Vietnamese Marines pulled back from their positions north of Quang Tri. Reconnoitring the road to that town were these BTR-40A armoured cars. (PAVN)

Leading the PAVN battalions converging on Quang Tri were the T-54s of the 7th Company of the 203rd Brigade. They soon entered the city unopposed; the local RF defenders having fled at the appearance of the North Vietnamese tanks. (PAVN)

It took the North Vietnamese several days to send their forces against the northern defence perimeter of Hue after the fall of Quang Tri. These ATS-59 tracked artillery tractors are seen crossing the Thach Han River on a barge. (PAVN)

Accompanying the North Vietnamese columns converging against Hue's northern perimeter were these S-60 57mm anti-aircraft guns, towed by Chinese built CA-30 trucks. (PAVN)

Despite Truong's caution, Thieu went ahead with his speech on 20 March. Speaking on the media, the President was short on specifics. He remained vague and did not deliver the forceful denunciation of a secret deal to partition the land that civilians and military alike needed to raise their morale. However, he reaffirmed his will to defend the rest of the country, particularly Hue, until the end.

Returning from an inspection trip at Hue, Truong landed back at Da Nang on the evening of 20 March, just to hear President Thieu's speech on TV, with his pledge to defend Hue whatever the cost. Upon arriving at his headquarters, he found a cable from the JGS awaiting him. The message, flown to Da Nang by special courier, was a bombshell. It stated: "Limited air and naval resources available are only sufficient to support one enclave. You are therefore to conduct a delaying action by withdrawing to the Hai Van Pass if the situation permits". Despite the earlier agreement with Thieu to fight for Hue, a stunned Truong interpreted the cable to mean that he was to abandon the city and retreat to Da Nang. Shortly thereafter, a second cable arrived from JGS countermanding Thieu's permission to retain the Airborne brigade. Enormously upset, Truong, probably the ARVN's most brilliant tactician, penned a quick reply to JGS: "I feel weak and confused. I am afraid I am not capable of carrying out my duties. I request that you accept my resignation".

After receiving Truong's resignation cable, Thieu immediately clarified his message. His intend had been to provide Truong the flexibility to deal with the situation, not to give the impression that

to defend the land. Thieu agreed, but on the condition that the Airborne not be used in combat.

he had abruptly changed his mind about Hue. While temporarily mollified, Truong knew he still faced major difficulties. In addition to the crumbling of his northern front, he was now confronted by a new offensive south of Hue. The PAVN plan called for the B4 Front to attack the Marines defending the Bo River northwest of Hue while concurrently sending forces across the My Chanh River. South of Hue, the 324th Division would again strike the Bong and Mo Tau Mountains and Hill 224, with the support of two tank battalions of the 203rd Armoured Brigade in the second echelon. Simultaneously, the 325th Division would cut Route 1 to prevent ARVN troops from retreating to Da Nang. The unit was ordered to attack on schedule on 21 March and would cut Route 1 no matter what the cost. The unit had spent a month to prepare its

The 258th Marine Brigade, after retreating from Quang Tri sector, settled in temporarily along the My Chan River. It was there that the Marines had already stopped the North Vietnamese three years earlier during the Easter Offensive of 1972. However, this time, they were ordered to pull back and tried to retreat to Da Nang. (ARVN)

starting attack positions, including eight separate camouflaged artillery positions, with twenty-four 105mm and 122mm howitzers of its organic 84th Artillery Regiment, positioned on a series of hills. Facing the 325th Division were the 60th and 61st Battalions of the 15th Ranger Group deployed on Hill 560 and Hill 312 in the Mom Kum Sac Mountain range. Once the hills were overrun, Route 1 was only 2km away. Hue would be cut off, and thousands of South Vietnamese soldiers and civilians would be trapped.

The North Vietnamese offensive started at dawn on 21 March. The Communist artillery barrage pounded the Rangers' positions before moving to Phu Loc and even to some ships in nearby waters. The assault was led by the 18th Regiment, 325th Division, against Hill 560. Its 101st Regiment struck Hill 312. Within an hour, the Communists had captured several strong points near Hill 560, but the hill remained in the Rangers' hands. They were supported by several 105mm artillery batteries along Route 1. The defenders of Hill 560 pushed back another assault after hand-to-hand fighting. The North Vietnamese discovered a near vertical slope protected by a minefield where they infiltrated troops and surprised the South Vietnamese from the rear. By early afternoon, Hill 560 was taken. The 101st Regiment was less successful against Hill 312, the Rangers resisting furiously. But with the fall of Hill 560, the whole 15th Ranger Group was ordered to pull back to regroup. The PAVN gunners now pounded the heavily congested Route 1, hitting many military and civilian vehicles alike. That night three battalions of the 325th Division pushed towards the road, cleared the RF bunkers and occupied a 3km stretch of road. The South Vietnamese immediately reacted, trying to clear out the roadblock, with the 8th Marine Battalion and the 94th Ranger Battalion, 15th Group, attacking from both sides the entrenched North Vietnamese. Despite heavy air support, the counterattack failed, sealing the fate of Hue. Although the troops of the 325th Division had now been awake for 48 hours, Giap offered them no respite. In a message on the afternoon of 22 March, he commended the 325th Division's cutting of Route 1 as a "tremendous achievement". However, the division had to maintain a firm grip on the newly captured section of Route 1, no matter what the cost. During the night, the whole division moved to Route 1, accompanied by a dozen T-54s of the 4th

A mortar crew manning a 120mm mortar opening fire against the ARVN outposts along the Mom Kum Sac Mountain range south of Hue in support of the PAVN 325th Division's attack to cut Route 1. (PAVN)

The PAVN 325th Division's drive towards the coast south of Hue to cut Route 1 was supported by its own organic 84th Artillery Regiment. The unit was also strengthened by a dozen Type 63 105mm MRLs. (PAVN

On 22 March, the PAVN's 325th Division had grabbed a portion of Route 1 south of Hue, with the support of a dozen T-54s of the 4th Battalion, 203rd Armoured Brigade. (PAVN)

Company, 4th Tank Battalion. At dawn, the North Vietnamese occupied a stretch 10km-long along Route 1 between the Mui Ne promontory and the bridge of Bai Son.

Meanwhile, simultaneously to the offensive of the 325th Division, the 324th Division struck Hills 224 and 303, and the Bong and Mo Tau Mountains. It was supported by the rest of the 4th Tank Battalion. The T-54s had left their parking area at A Loui on 21 March before moving up Route 74, a bad mountain track where several tanks bogged down. On 23 March, they crossed the Vung Tran River before bypassing the Bong Mountains and Nui Nghe to be kept at disposal of the 324th Division. Within a short time, Hill 224 was captured, but the PAVN advance was halted at Hill 303. On Bong Mountain, the ARVN 1st Regiment, 1st Division, was pushed back, but a counterattack reclaimed the high ground. Savage fighting continued to roil across Bong Mountain, which changed hands multiple times. Finally, on the morning of 23 March, the 1st Regiment regained control of the mountain. On Mo Tau, the ARVN 54th

The PAVN's 324th Division was finally ordered to bypass the Mo Tau sector and attacked towards the coastal area to join forces with the 325th Division. Both divisions were supported by two battalions of T-54s of the 203rd Armoured Brigade. (PAVN)

Troops of the PAVN's 324th Division boarding ZIL-130 and ZIL-157 trucks to attack down the coastal lowlands south of Hue on 21 March 1975. (PAVN)

Simultaneously to the PAVN 325th Division's attack to cut Route 1 south of Hue, the 324th Division also resumed its attacks against the Mo Tau and Bong Mountains held by the ARVN 1st Division. This North Vietnamese BS-3 100mm anti-tank gun is firing against a South Vietnamese fortified position. (PAVN)

Regiment, 1st Division, repulsed several assaults. The 1st Division had held once more but the 324th Division's assault prevented the 1st Division from assisting the 15th Ranger Group on its flank.

However, with Route 1 now cut, Brigadier General An decided to shift strategy. He ordered the 324th Division to bypass the 1st Division and penetrate directly into the lowlands with the tanks of the 4th Battalion. Concurrently, the 325th Division would resume the attack and send one regiment north of Route 1 towards the

15th Rangers' headquarters at Luong Dien. Once that last place was captured, the regiment would attack Phu Bai airport in coordination with the 324th Division. The 325th Division's other regiments would strike Phu Loc. On the night of 22 March, the 324th Division left one regiment behind to pin down the ARVN 1st Division and sent its two other regiments to attack Hue from the south. With T-54s in support, the 324th Division reached Route 1. After regrouping its forces, refuelling its vehicles and picking up its supporting artillery, the 324th Division attacked towards Phu Loc but the South Vietnamese blew up the bridge at the entry of the town.

Facing these serious developments, Lieutenant General Thi needed to stop a PAVN thrust into the undefended land south of Hue. Consequently, on the night of 22 March he pulled in his defences. He ordered the 15th Ranger Group to withdraw across the Truoi River, while the 1st and 54th Regiments, 1st Division, were told to withdraw from their hilltops and moved closer to Hue's south-western flank. Together they would form a new defensive line to protect Hue's soft underbelly. The 1st Division's other two regiments would remain in their positions west of the city.

That afternoon, Truong received another distressing message from the JGS, indicating that Saigon was capable of supporting only one enclave. For this reason, by every means possible, Truong should form only an enclave at Da Nang. During the initial phase, the 1st Division, 3rd Division, and the Marine Division would move into the Da Nang enclave. In phase two, the 2nd Division would move into the enclave as well. When the entire 2nd Division had arrived, Truong was ordered to immediately return the Marine Division to the National Level Command Authority. This was the final blow for the ARVN I Corps. Whatever President Thieu's intent, upon receipt of these orders, Truong ordered the 8th Marine Battalion to cease its efforts to reopen Route 1, and to established positions closer to the Hai Van Pass. With the main escape route towards Da Nang closed, Truong ordered the 1st Division to hold out against the North Vietnamese, allowing time for the retrieval by sea, first of the precious Marines, and as well as a maximum of heavy equipment. The 1st Division would be the last to be retrieved.

But the North Vietnamese offered no respite to Truong. Giap ordered the B4 Front not to stop at the My Chanh River but instead continue to attack, coordinating its efforts with the 2nd SAC to capture Hue. Facing the B4 Front, the ARVN had positioned the 14th Ranger Group and the remnant of the Quang Tri Province RF, along with the 7th Marine Battalion, to guard the area from the bridge on Route 1 over the My Chanh River east to the sea. An 18km front was being covered by fewer than 2,000 men. Elements of the ARVN I Armoured Brigade were

With the deterioration of the situation around Hue, some of the troops and refugees were evacuated by sea on 21 March towards Da Nang. That included heavy equipment like these M107 175mm SP guns. (US Navy)

A requisitioned civilian ship fully loaded with troops evacuated from Hue towards Da Nang on 23 March. (US Navy)

arrayed along the western side of the bridge along the My Chanh River to the mountains, and then south to Hue. The ARVN 1st Division was deployed from west of Hue south along the mountains down to the Truoi River, where the 15th Ranger Group took over from the river to Phu Loc. The 8th Marine Battalion held Phu Loc, and a Thua Thien Province RF Group guarded the Hai Van Pass area. This left Lieutenant General Thi of the I Corps Forward with no reserve to call upon if his lines were penetrated.

The B4 Front planned its main assault against the RF positions near the coast. It mobilised three Quang Tri local force battalions positioned on the eastern side of Route 1, and the reinforced 4th Regiment on the western side. It would send two Quang Tri local forces battalions, supported by the 7th Tank Company, to puncture the RF lines and capture the district capital of Huong Dien. It would then continue south along the coastline and strike the ports of Thuan An – Tan My, the only remaining escape route for the South Vietnamese units trapped in the Hue pocket. The Thuan An – Tan My harbour area and warehouse facilities were located next to the coast on the Perfume River about 8km east of Hue. Only small ships could sail into Hue and although Tan My had several LST ramps, silting prevented the LSTs from entering the harbour. Lack of funds had prevented the dredging of the access channel. The port of Tan My was connected to the port at Thuan An by a floating bridge across the Tam Giang Lagoon.

The PAVN local force 3rd Battalion would attack near the bridge on Route 1, while the 4th Regiment would attack the 147th Marine

Brigade. The independent 46th Regiment, recently arrived from North Vietnam, constituted the second echelon with the Front's 16th Artillery Regiment. The two other B4 Front regiments, the 6th and 271st Regiments and although badly battered from earlier fighting, were southwest of Hue and prepared to strike from that direction. Concurrently with these attacks, the B4 Front ordered the 5th and 13th Thua Thien local force battalions to cut off and control Thu Hien Inlet, "no matter what the cost". On the night of 22 March, the two battalions slipped by ARVN outposts and marched to a position on the coast just south of the inlet. The next night, they crossed Cau Hai Bay and began firing at the naval base located at Tu Hien Inlet with ZIS-2 57mm and D-44 85mm guns of the attached 6th Artillery Battalion.

Meanwhile, on 21 March, the newly set up 468th Marine Brigade arrived from Saigon and replaced the 1st Airborne Brigade at the Hai Van Pass. In fact, the unit had only two battalions, the third was retained at Da Nang for further training. The 258th Marine Brigade headquarters soon departed the pass but left the 8th Marine Battalion behind. The newly arrived unit, instead of being engaged in the reopening the vital Route 1 was just occupying defensive positions protecting the Hue enclave that in the end had to be abandoned. More incredible, the brigade was deployed while the next day the JGS ordered the pull-out of the Marine Division from the I Corps. Obviously, signs of panic began to appear at the highest ARVN echelons of command.

Pressure on the northern perimeter increased as the hours passed by. On 22 March, at 3:00 p.m. the 4th Regiment launched its attack and caught a Marine battalion off guard. The North Vietnamese cut off two platoons and pushed back the Marine defences. Being outflanked, Marine Colonel Nguyen Van Thi ordered a retreat back to the final defence of Hue, along the Bo River. Thi attempted to send a Marine company and tanks to support the RF, but the North Vietnamese began shelling the 147th Marine Brigade's positions, halting that plan. In mid-afternoon, the remaining RF collapsed and began streaming back to the final defensive line north of Hue behind the An Lo Bridge on the Bo River, only 30km from the city. That night the cut-off platoons escaped and linked up with their parent unit. Tri deployed the 14th Ranger Group from the An Lo Bridge to Thuan An Lagoon, while pulling the 7th Marine Battalion back to defend Huong Dien. The 147th Brigade retreated behind the Bo River.

On 23 March, the PAVN resumed their attacks, overwhelming South Vietnamese defences on the Bo River without much resistance, the Quang Tri 913th RF Group had virtually disintegrated as a fighting force. Most of the RF troops had deserted to find their families despite the Marine officers and province officials trying to stop them. The Communists captured the districts of Quang Dien, Quang Loi and Hương Can. The North Vietnamese immediately positioned a battery of M-46 130mm long-range guns at Cua Thuan to pound Hue but after firing just 360 rounds, the ARVN counterbattery fires neutralised the guns. However, that pounding started panic among the inhabitants who rushed in mass to Thuan An port, compounding the chaos that already reigned there with many civilian and military vehicles crowding the piers.

The B4 Front now pressed on, sending the 4th, 46th and 271st Regiments pursuing a retreating South Vietnamese formation consisting of the 147th Marine Brigade, the 14th Ranger Group, the 5th Infantry Regiment, 1st Infantry Division, and the 17th ACS, heading towards Thuan An. The North Vietnamese were supported by PT-76 and T-54 tanks of the 2nd Armoured Battalion, as well as 18 M-46 130mm and D-74 122mm long-range guns of the B4

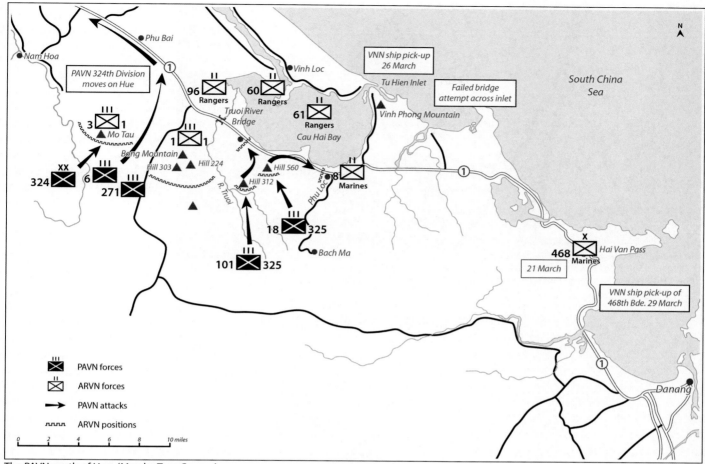

The PAVN south of Hue. (Map by Tom Cooper)

Front's 16th Artillery Regiment. The unit had been rushed to the scene from its storage area at Ben Kham. Its tracked artillery tractors drove over rough terrain, including an area pocketed by craters due to previous B-52s carpet bombing.

Meanwhile, on 23 March, the North Vietnamese also resumed the attack south of Hue. The 325th Division sent its three regiments to attack in opposite directions along Route 1. The previous day, one battalion from the 101st Regiment was mauled taking a hill from the 15th Ranger Group, but still manage to capture it. This placed the 101st Regiment to assault the Ranger base at Luong Dien. Taking Luong Dien would outflank ARVN forces defending Hill 303 and Mo Tau.

On the morning of 23 March, the101st Regiment assaulted Luong Dien. After a day-long battle, the Rangers retreated over the Truoi River and blew up the bridge behind them and withdrew to Phu Bai AB. At 4:30 a.m., the 3rd and 101st Regiments, with the 4th Tank Battalion in the lead, launched an attack against the airbase. But the tanks found the bridge at An Nong already destroyed, forcing them to detour via Moc Chau, before heading towards Phu Bai AB. The attack resumed only the next morning, but the enemy had already vacated the airfield where the north Vietnamese captured three intact M48 tanks and a dozen M113s that were immediately pressed into service by the PAVN's 203rd Armoured Brigade. Meanwhile, on the other flank, the 325th Division's 18th Regiment overran Phu Loc after the 8th Marine Battalion pulled out following a spirited fight. The Marines knocked out seven T-54 tanks of the 4th Company, 4th Tank Battalion, with their M72 LAW rockets.

To pin down the ARVN 1st Division, the remaining 324th Division regiment simultaneously attacked Hill 303 and Bong Mountain. The ARVN positions held out until a tank attack in the afternoon finally captured the two positions. With his defences south of Hue being compressed, the 1st Division commander ordered his two regiments defending the Mo Tau – Bong Mountain – Hill 303 complex to retreat to Phu Bai. While extracting his troops from the area, Brigadier General Diem learned that Phu Bai AB was already encircled by the 325th Division and on the verge of being taken. He then decided on a general pull-out of his remaining two regiments west of Hue closer to the city. On the same day, Trung ordered the CO of I Corps Forward, Lieutenant General Lam Quang Thi to meet him in Da Nang. When Thi arrived, Truong ordered him to continue defending Hue, but also to draft contingency plans to withdraw his forces to Da Nang. In discussing this possibility, Thi laid out his design. He wanted the Navy to sink ships across the 80m wide Tu Hien Inlet, and the Marines to secure Vinh Phong Mountain, which dominated the southern side of the inlet. Then the 1st Division, Thua Thien RF, and the 15th Ranger Group would march across the ships and link up with the Marines, thereby bypassing the roadblock at Phu Loc. The forces north of Hue would retreat to Tan My port and be picked up by Navy ships.

Thi immediately flew back to Hue and spent 23 March preparing the move. He began by shifting his headquarters out of Hue to the Thuan An naval base. On 24 March he called a meeting of his top-ranking officers who described the grim situation. Hue was abandoned, thousands of civilians and vehicles were clogging the road to Tan My, the 1st Division was under pressure. Given wavering troop morale and no reserves, they concluded that defending Hue was hopeless. Worse, the CO of the 1st Division stated that if they did not move immediately, the PAVN would soon punch through his lines and attack Tan My. At best they had a day before his lines collapsed.

By 23 March, the PAVN resumed its offensive against the crumbling Hue enclave. An AT-S tracked artillery tractor of the 16th Artillery Regiment moved in with an M-46 130mm gun to support the attack against the northern sector. (PAVN)

The North Vietnamese positioned their 130mm long-range artillery to pound Thuan An harbour, sealing the last escape route from Hue. (PAVN)

Fleet with its seagoing ships. The frigates and destroyers would create a screen stretching for 10 miles around Thuan An Inlet to guard against North Vietnamese torpedo and patrol boats that might attempt to disrupt the evacuation, or to lay mines near the narrow entrance. Twenty-two landing craft from the Army's Military Transportation Command were also placed under the Navy's control and ordered to ferry people out to the larger ships.

On 24 March the naval base at Tu Hien was charged with lashing several craft together so the 1st Division could cross, but the effort failed because the current was too swift. Sinking a ship was also determined to be unfeasible, so the Navy decided to tow a floating bridge from Da Nang. When the floating bridge finally arrived, enemy shelling with 85mm guns from Vinh Phong Mountain made its deployment impossible. For some unknown reason, the Marines had failed to secure the high ground despite Lieutenant General Thi's repeated requests.

North of Hue on the morning of 24 March, the PAVN 4th Regiment crossed the Bo River in two places and assaulted the Marines, but they held their ground. To support the Marines, the 14th Ranger Group, backed by M41 tanks, counterattacked several times, but they did not succeed in destroying the two bridgeheads. After the decision in the late afternoon of 24 March to withdraw from Hue, the Marines were ordered to retreat. The rest of the 1st Armoured Brigade and the 14th Ranger Group acted as rear guard. After the Marines left, the Rangers retreated and blew up the An Lo Bridge behind them. After receiving sporadic artillery fire at Thuan An naval base, around 6:30 p.m., Lieutenant General Thi, CO of I Corps Forward, and his staff boarded a Navy ship. At this point, Thi lost control of his units. Worse, upon returning from his meeting with Truong, Brigadier General Diem gathered his staff for a final conference. While there remains confusion as to his exact orders, instead of leading the 1st Division in its most critical hours, Diem disbanded his unit and told his officers to make their own way to the pick-up point at Tu Hien. While the 1st Division had fought valiantly to this point, by midnight of 24 March, it had collapsed. Truong had hoped that the 1st Division that had long been associated with the defence of Hue, and where many of the families of the soldiers lived, would energetically defend the city by covering the evacuation. In reality, men and officers while

The decision was made to have the Marines retreat to Tan My, cross the inlet, and then move along the beach away from the civilians to a pick-up point about 5km south. The 14th Ranger Group and elements of the 1st Armoured Brigade would fight a rear-guard action and then join the Marines. The 1st Division would move to Thu Hien Inlet, with the 15th Ranger Group and Thua Thien RF screening the beachhead. All supplies and heavy equipment, including artillery and tanks, would be destroyed. Brigadier General Dien told Thi that only two of his four regiments would be able to escape. The CO of the 1st Division then flew to Da Nang to present the withdrawal plan to Truong. Meeting with Truong, Diem categorically stated that the defence of Hue was impossible, so at 6:00 p.m. on 24 March, Truong ordered the evacuation. Truong then called President Thieu, who agreed that Hue would be evacuated. Diem flew back to deliver the news to Thi.

Truong's naval commander, Commodore Ho Van Ky Thoai, was ordered to prepare for the evacuation of Hue. The Navy headquarters in Saigon also committed every asset available, including the Sea

pulling back, deserted en masse in search of their loved ones. Once more time, the "family syndrome" engulfed another ARVN unit, many searching for a means to escape south as everyone was persuaded that the government had decided to abandon the northern half of the country. Diem's dissolution of the division doomed the Hue pocket, opening the southern perimeter to the North Vietnamese. Why Diem, a native of Hue who had served with distinction in the 1st Division, disbanded his unit was unknown: he died several days later in a helicopter crash.

T-54s of the 4th Battalion of the 203rd Armoured Brigade moved on towards the southern perimeter of Hue on 25 March 1975. (PAVN)

Despite the mobs at the ports, the landing craft continued to shuttle people from Tan My out to the LSTs. They rescued about 6,000 civilians on 24 March. While the evacuation continued that night, rough seas and enemy shelling were making it increasingly hazardous. By midnight, over half of the landing craft had abandoned the rescue and withdrawn to Da Nang.

Marching almost 30km that night, by the morning of 25 March the exhausted Marines had gathered on the beach several kilometres south of Thuan An port. After the Marines formed a defensive perimeter, the headquarters of the 147th Marine Brigade boarded a small transport ship and moved offshore. The 1st Armoured Brigade was forced to abandon much of its equipment several kilometres

The North Vietnamese moved in a battery of BM-14-17 MRLs to pound the Thuan An embarkation point. Firing salvos of seventeen 140mm rockets, they caused considerable destruction. (PAVN)

from Tan My. Thousands of other troops, including RF/PF, logistic, and engineers, jammed the piers. Communist shelling hit them, buildings were burning, the dead littered the streets. Joining the guns of the B4 Front's 16th Artillery Regiment were those of the 164th Artillery Brigade of the 2nd SAC, firing from the southern Hue perimeter.

The Navy shifted from the ports to the beach in order to rescue the Marines, but heavy waves prevented the small landing boats from coming ashore. At 1:30 p.m., the order was given to the LST *Can Tho* (HQ-801) to beach. The ship could only get within 100m of the shore, where she halted and dropped rope ladders over the sides. While the Marines had maintained unit discipline, ARVN troops had not. Several thousand civilians and leaderless soldiers had followed the Marines. The ship boarding turned into a mad

rush with people struggling through the waves to wade towards the rescuing ship. Some M113 APCs tried their chance by swimming over the heads of the unfortunates that were in their path. With the current growing stronger, after less than an hour, the *Can Tho* reversed engines and pulled back to avoid becoming grounded.

The Marines decided to shift further south along the beach to avoid the mobs of soldiers and civilians. After marching south nearly 2km, the Marines spread out and dug foxholes in the sand. They expelled any refugees and soldiers trying to enter their perimeter, shooting several peoples they considered Communist infiltrators. It was the first crack in the vaunted Marines discipline. The VNN ships, however, had no better luck finding a suitable landing area in the new position.

A general view of Thuan An, the port of Hue, shows the havoc caused on the amassed ARVN vehicles waiting to embark on ships by enemy artillery. (PAVN)

PAVN artillery also inflicted heavy losses on the ARVN vehicles awaiting on the other side of Tam Giang Lagoon at Tan My port, connected to Thuan An port by a floating bridge. (PAVN)

A closer view among the destroyed ARVN equipment at Tan My port, including in the foreground an M42 anti-aircraft artillery tank. (PAVN)

Meanwhile, the North Vietnamese pushed towards Thuan An, with the 4th Regiment advancing west of Hue. The 8th Battalion crossed the Bo River on Route 1 and by 9:00 a.m. of 25 March had captured a district town only 5km outside Hue. It then sent a reconnaissance element on trucks and in BTR-40s to seize another bridge on the city's edge. At the bridge, they were met by two underground Viet Cong agents that announced to them that ARVN had abandoned Hue. Guided by the Viet Cong agents, they entered the city unopposed. At 10:30 a.m. the North Vietnamese raised their flag over the Hue Citadel, on the same flagpole many of the ARVN 1st Division had died retaking in 1968. At noon, advance elements of the 3rd Regiment, 324th Division, with T-54s and captured M48s and M113s, entered Hue from the south. Continuing their advance towards the ocean, B4 Front units, and the 2nd Regiment, 324th Division,

These three ARVN M48 tanks were captured intact near the Phu Bai airbase. They were promptly put into service with the 203rd Armoured Brigade. (PAVN)

On 26 March 1975, a group of North Vietnamese soldiers symbolically run through one of the gates of the Imperial Palace of Hue when the Communist forces entered unopposed the ancient imperial capital. (PAVN)

The North Vietnamese captured much abandoned ARVN equipment in the Hue enclave, including this M41 tank near the Imperial Palace. (PAVN)

which was moving towards Tan My, linked up at around 5:00 p.m. Both ports had now been captured.

Lieutenant General Thi, learning that Thuan An was under enemy fire and that the Navy had not erected the bridge across the inlet mouth, ordered the ships to proceed south to pick up the troops stranded there. The vast majority of VNN ships departed Hue at 4:45 p.m. With the arrival of the Navy ships at Tu Hien, south of Phu Bai AB, at around midnight 25 March, the small landing crafts began shuttling troops. By dawn, they managed to rescue about 1,100 soldiers. One 1st Division regiment had arrived at the Tu Hien Inlet, but the naval officer commanding the coastal squadron moved his ships out to sea after an Army officer pulled out his pistol and threatened to kill him if he did not transport his troops to the other side. Now stranded, some soldiers stole local fishing boats while others attempted to swim across the inlet. Many drowned in the swift currents.

With the bulk of the Navy at Tu Hien, Truong arranged for three other landing craft to beach at dawn, 26 March, to rescue the 4,000 stranded Marines. The wounded and the dead would be loaded first, then the 147th Brigade headquarters, and then the rest of the

Marines. The 7th VNMC Battalion would hold the line and board last. When the first landing craft hit the beach that morning, the Marines loaded in an orderly fashion, but after an hour, elements of the PAVN 1st Regiment, 324th Division, arrived. The North Vietnamese fired an AT-3 Sagger anti-tank missile that hit the ship, wounding the brigade commander. Fearful of more missiles, the ship quickly backed away. Only 800 Marines had made it onboard. To avoid the encroaching enemy, the Marines again moved south of the beach.

Around noon, another landing craft beached. This time, Marine discipline gave way. Hundreds of men swarmed the ship, and it became overloaded and stuck in the sand. Many of the trailing civilians and soldiers also tried to rush onboard. Since the Marines had been told this ship was reserved for them, they began shooting people to rid themselves of the weight. This total collapse of Marine discipline would manifest itself again in Da Nang. As the ship lay immobilised, the PAVN gunners suddenly found the range. Several rounds hit the ship, wounding and killing dozens. Realising they were sitting ducks, a Marine battalion commander ordered everyone off. As the bow door opened, Communist machinegun fire cut down dozens more. The remaining Marines desperately dug

PAVN soldiers entered the devastated port at Thuan An, looking for what could be salvaged from the destroyed equipment. (PAVN)

The North Vietnamese also found these abandoned vehicles along Route 1 south of Hue, including an M48 tank. (PAVN)

troops moved south along the beach. Very few Marines made it to Tu Hien, and most were captured the next day. Many committed suicide with grenades rather than surrender.

PAVN figures for South Vietnamese losses in the Hue pocket were staggering, they claimed they captured 58,722 South Vietnamese soldiers, with one colonel and 18 lieutenant-colonels amongst the ranks, as well as about 14,000 South Vietnamese government officials and employees, who reported to the Communist authorities. In addition to the 147th Marine Brigade, the 1st Division, the 14th and 15th Ranger Groups, part of the 1st Armoured Brigade, several artillery battalions, and 15 RF battalions were destroyed. Equipment losses were enormous. The Communists captured for their own use 140 tanks and APCs, 800 trucks, and 10,000 tons of ammunition. Only 16,000 ARVN soldiers of the I Corps Forward managed to reach Da Nang.

defensive positions and tried to fight back, but they were almost out of ammunition. As night fell, the firefight with North Vietnamese troops continued. The Marines had nowhere to hide, and the senior commanders decided they had no choice but tried and fought their way to the Tu Hien crossing. Forming a column, the remaining

5
DISASTER AT DA NANG

While the northern I Corps area was collapsing with the fall of Quang Tri and Hue, the situation also deteriorated in its southern sector. At the start of the campaign, the directives for the PAVN B1 Front which covered that part of the theatre were to capture Tien Phuoc and eliminated several ARVN battalions. Now, the CO of the B1 Front sensed an opportunity to destroy the entire ARVN 2nd Division and capture all of Quang Ngai Province. The commander of the South Vietnamese 2nd Division, Brigadier General Tran Van Nhut had recently pulled his units back to screen the populated lowlands and major cities. In a line running south from northern Quang Tin to the Binh Dinh Province border, a distance of 145km, Nhut had the 5th Regiment and the 12th Ranger Group defending Tam Ky, the 4th Regiment at Chu Lai, and the 6th Regiment and the 11th Ranger Group in Quang Ngai City. The B1 Front's new design called for a major attack against Tam Ky by the PAVN 2nd Division that would draw the ARVN 2nd Division forces to defend the city, whereupon they would be surrounded and cut off. The PAVN 52nd Brigade would then attack Quang Ngai as their ultimate objective. The offensive would be supported by the 574th Armoured Regiment equipped with Type 63, T-34/85, and T-54 tanks. The unit had just been reinforced by a company of K-63 APCs but lacked enough crew members to man all the vehicles. Consequently, a number of tank crews were hastily trained to man them. The regiment had left its rear depot areas arrayed in the Nuoc Sa Valley to be engaged in the support of an attack against Tam Ky. The B1 Front also lent its 572nd and 576th Artillery Regiments in support.

On 21 March, D-44 85mm and BS-3 100mm guns of the 368th Artillery Regiment, organic to the PAVN 2nd Division, began blasting away at RF positions around Tam Ky. Nhut reacted to the attack precisely as the B1 Front hoped: he moved the 4th Regiment from Chu Lai to reinforce Tam Ky, and he pulled a battalion from the 6th Regiment to protect Chu Lai. But the newly deployed troops saw their morale rapidly sinking. The men learned of the bloody retreat from the Central Highlands and, closer to home, the desperate situation in Hue and the growing refugee problem in Da Nang where many of their families lived.

By 7:00 am on 24 March, the cities of Tam Ky and Quang Ngai were simultaneously attacked by the PAVN after a heavy artillery barrage. The 2nd Division concentrated against the former, and the 52nd Brigade against the latter. The armour-led assault virtually destroyed the 39th Ranger Battalion in the outskirts of Tam Ky but encountered fierce resistance by the 37th Ranger battalion, 12th Group. After regrouping its forces, a

new attempt was made, with as a spearhead a "penetration group" constituted by the reinforced 2nd Tank Company with 10 T-54s, and 10 K-63s leading the 31st Regiment. The armoured task force supported an assault of the 31st Regiment, 2nd Division, amid a violent downpour that grounded VNAF aircraft. The tanks overwhelmed all the strong points and took the Tam Ky Bridge leading into the western entrance of the city. The T-54 of the company commander, Nguyen Quoc Vinh, which had just crossed the bridge saw its way blocked by an ARVN M113. Too close to take it out with its 100mm main gun, it opened fire against it with its 12.7mm HMG, before ramming the enemy vehicle. Now subdivided into three columns,

The PAVN 2nd SAC's new commander was Lieutenant General Le Trong Tan, just returned from a staff course in the Soviet Union. Considered one of the best North Vietnamese commanders of mechanized operations, he was also placed in charge of the assault against Da Nang at the head of the new Front 475. Tan would ultimately lead the last drive against Saigon by commanding the forces attacking the capital's eastern perimeter. (PAVN)

Deputy to Lieutenant General Le Trong Tan for the attack against Da Nang was Major General Chu Huy Man, fourth from left, CO of the PAVN's Military Region 5. He also acted as the Front Political Commissar. (PAVN)

The offensive against the Da Nang enclave started in its southern sector with attacks of the PAVN's 2nd Division and 52nd Brigade against Tam Ky and Quang Ngai City. They were supported by the 574th Armoured Regiment equipped with Type 63, T-54, and T-34/85 tanks, and T-34/85s like these two. (PAVN)

The 574th Armoured Regiment was reinforced with a company of K-63 APCs from January 1975. (PAVN)

the armour converged onto the local airfield, taking the ARVN western defence sector from behind. The rest of the PAVN 2nd Division poured into the breach and by midday Tam Ky was firmly in its hands. The ARVN 4th Regiment retreated and was pick up by helicopters on a nearby beach. The VNAF A-37s and F-5s pounded the enemy columns and slow them to close Route 1, allowing the 12th Ranger Group to escape north towards the Quang Nam Province border. The 5th Regiment and most of the RF however fled south to Chu Lai. The 36th Regiment, 2nd PAVN Division, tried to seal the escape route by capturing the Ba Bau Bridge but most of the ARVN troops had already passed through.

The ARVN resistance at Quang Ngai City was initially very stiff. A Ranger battalion, supported by a troop of M41 tanks of the 4th ACR, pushed back several uncoordinated assaults at Tuan Duong by the 52nd Brigade, reinforced by the 403rd and 406th Dac Cong Assault Sapper Battalions, and the local 94th Regiment. However, the 6th Regiment,

The PAVN's 2nd Division entered Tam Ky on 24 March 1975, riding Chinese built K-63 APCs and CA-30 trucks. (PAVN)

A camouflaged ARVN XM-706E2, a variant of the standard V100 Commando armoured car developed for the USAF for airbases security. This simplified version did not have a turret but instead an armoured parapet in its place and carried an M2 .50-cal machine gun. The South Vietnamese inherited a number of these when the United States left Southeast Asia in 1973. (Artwork by David Bocquelet)

The South Vietnamese standard tank was the M41 Walker Bulldog, equipping the tank troops of the Armoured Cavalry Squadrons (ACS). This vehicle belonged to the 7th ACS, the constituent armoured unit of the ARVN 1st Division operating near Hue in March 1975. (Artwork by David Bocquelet)

An ARVN M42 of the 3rd Anti-aircraft Artillery Battalion, operating in the Da Nang area in March 1975. It was, with 1st Anti-aircraft Artillery Battalion, one of the two battalions of this kind deployed in I Corps. Each battalion also operated a battery of M55 quad .50-cal machine guns mounted on M35 trucks, and a battery of M163 Vulcan 20mm guns. (Artwork by David Bocquelet)

An ARVN M48A3 tank of the 20th Tank Squadron, 1st Armoured Brigade. The unit constituted the main armoured reserve of I Corps, although it was mainly deployed north of the Hai Van Pass by 1975. (Artwork by David Bocquelet)

An ARVN M113 APC of the 4th ACS, the constituent armoured unit of the 2nd Division, Chu Lai, March 1975. This vehicle was later put into use by the North Vietnamese. (Artwork by David Bocquelet)

An ARVN M107 gun of the 102nd Artillery Battalion, one of the two artillery battalions of I Corps equipped with the self-propelled 175mm guns. The M107 was the only gun of the ARVN arsenal to be able to outrange the North Vietnamese M-46 130mm guns. (Artwork by David Bocquelet)

An ARVN M113 equipped with a BGM-71 TOW anti-tank guided missile, probably from the 17th ACS, 1st Armoured Brigade, Quang Tri, February 1975. South Vietnam was the first foreign customer of the TOW system when they were rushed into service during the Easter Offensive of the spring of 1972 to counter the North Vietnamese armour. (Artwork by David Bocquelet)

A PAVN GAZ-63 (4x4) 2-ton truck of the 325th Division, around Hue in March 1975. By this stage of the conflict, practically all the North Vietnamese divisions were motorised formations with their own transportation units, equipped with a variety of trucks delivered by communist states. (Artwork by David Bocquelet)

A PAVN BM-24-17 MRL of the 164th Artillery Brigade, 2nd SAC, on the southern Hue perimeter in March 1975. Mounted on a GAZ-63 truck chassis, this rocket launcher system fired a salvo of seventeen 140mm rockets, at a maximum range of 10,600 m. (Artwork by David Bocquelet)

The North Vietnamese captured a huge booty after the fall of the ARVN I Corps, including some 40 tanks that were quickly turned against their former owners. This captured M41A3, wearing the National Liberation Front flag, was integrated to the newly raised 675th Tank Battalion in Da Nang. Soon, the unit rolled down the coastal Route 1 towards Saigon. (Artwork by David Bocquelet)

A PAVN BTR-40A armoured reconnaissance car of the 203rd Armoured Brigade, 2nd SAC, in Da Nang in March 1975. It was armed with twin 14.5mm heavy machine guns. (Artwork by David Bocquelet)

A PAVN ATS-59G tracked artillery tractor of the 576th Artillery Regiment, B1 Front, Thuong Duc sector, February 1975. The tracked vehicle was used to tow medium and heavy artillery pieces along mountainous tracks. (Artwork by David Bocquelet)

A PAVN BTR-60PB of the 202nd Armoured Brigade, 1st SAC. The North Vietnamese strategic reserve was finally committed at the end of March 1975 to participate in the final offensive against Saigon. The Corps had moved down the entire length of the Ho Chi Minh Trail in only two weeks. (Artwork by David Bocquelet)

A PAVN ZIL-131(6x6) 3 ½-Ton truck of Logistic Army 559 that ferried supplies and troops along the Ho Chi Minh Trail in March 1975. It was part of a batch of more modern trucks delivered by the Soviets in 1974, complementing the GAZ-53s, ZIL-130s, and ZIL-157s. (Artwork by David Bocquelet)

An SA-2 (S-75) missile trailer, with a ZIL-131V tractor, of the 274th SAM Regiment, 675th Anti-Aircraft Artillery Division, Da Nang, March 1975. (Artwork by David Bocquelet)

Lieutenant General Ngo Quang Truong, Commanding Officer of ARVN I Corps, looking over an M16 rifle of a soldier during an inspection tour. Truong was considered as one the best South Vietnamese tacticians but could not stem the North Vietnamese onslaught when he was deprived of both the Airborne and Marine Divisions. Contradictory orders given to him by President Nguyen Van Thieu caused additional confusion in his defensive plans. (Artwork by Anderson Subtil)

A South Vietnamese Marine private of the VNMC 369th Brigade, Quang Tri, March 1975. (Artwork by Anderson Subtil)

A private of the PAVN's 126th Naval Infantry Regiment, March 1975. The unit, specialised in amphibious operations, was engaged in the assault against Da Nang. It was later sent to occupy the group of islands occupied by the South Vietnamese in the Spratly Archipelago. (Artwork by Anderson Subtil)

A VNAF Cessna A-37B of one of the three Dragonfly squadrons of the 61st Tactical Wing at Da Nang. This particular aircraft, fully loaded with two M117 750lb, four Mk 82 500lb, and two Mk 81 250lb bombs, was preparing for a new sortie against the approaching North Vietnamese when it was damaged on its right wing by enemy tanks entering the airbase. The pilot, who jumped out of the cockpit at the entrance of the runway, was taken prisoner. (Artwork by Tom Cooper)

A VNAF A-37B of the 524th Fighter Squadron, 92nd Tactical Wing, Phan Rang AB, early April 1975. The fighter squadrons of this wing played an important role by delaying the advance of the North Vietnamese columns driving down south along the coastal Route 1 or moving down the Central Highlands along route 14. (Artwork by Tom Cooper)

The VNAF's 61st Tactical Wing at Da Nang had on its strength a squadron each of F-5As and F-Es. They were reinforced by rotational detachments of F-5s from the 63rd Tactical Wing at Bien Hoa, including this rare F-5C of the 542nd Fighter Squadron in air defence configuration, armed with AIM-9B Sidewinder air-to-air missiles. The threat of air attacks carried out by North Vietnamese combat aircraft against the overcrowded airbase forced VNAF to maintain aircraft for combat air patrols on alert. (Artwork by Tom Cooper)

A VNAF AC-119K of the 821st Attack Squadron, Da Nang, March 1975. The unit maintained, alongside the AC-119Gs of the 819th Attack Squadron, various detachments throughout the country. The main airbase for the gunships was however Tan Son Nhut, near Saigon. (Artwork by Tom Cooper)

A VNAF C-130A of the 437th Transport Squadron, 53rd Tactical Wing, Tan Son Nhut AB. With the 435th Transport Squadron, the two squadrons equipped with Hercules were fully mobilised by early 1975 despite maintenance problems. In addition to being involved in various transport missions, they were also used as makeshift bombers. This particular aircraft would be destroyed at Tan Son Nhut on 29 April 1975 by North Vietnamese artillery. (Artwork by Tom Cooper)

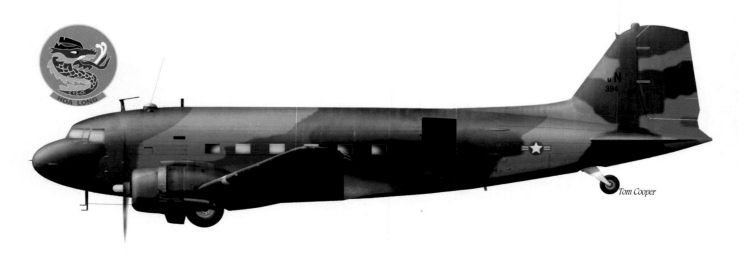

A VNAF AC-47D of the 817th Attack Squadron, March 1975. By that date, the gunships of the unit had seen their miniguns removed, being too vulnerable to be engaged in night attack missions. Instead, the squadron reverted to being a transport unit. (Artwork by Tom Cooper)

A VNAF UH-1H of the 51st Tactical Wing, Da Nang, March 1975. The helicopter wing of the 1st Air Division of Da Nang had on strength some five UH-1H squadrons and one CH-47A squadron. This particular helicopter was captured intact by the North Vietnamese. (Artwork by Luca Canossa)

A Boeing 727C of World Airways. This company, based in Oakland, California, was contracted by the US government to evacuate refugees from Da Nang, beginning from 25 March 1975. The chaotic situation at the local airport forced the cancellation of the air bridge after four days. The last B 727 took off with a record 330 passengers on board. (Artwork by Tom Cooper)

An Air America C-46F seen at Da Nang, March 1975. The Central Intelligence Agency-operated airline still used three C-46s in South Vietnam, alongside Caribous, C-47s, Volpars, and helicopters. They were intensively involved in the various evacuations of the abandoned cities. The C-46 frequently took off with over 100 refugees onboard. (Artwork by Tom Cooper)

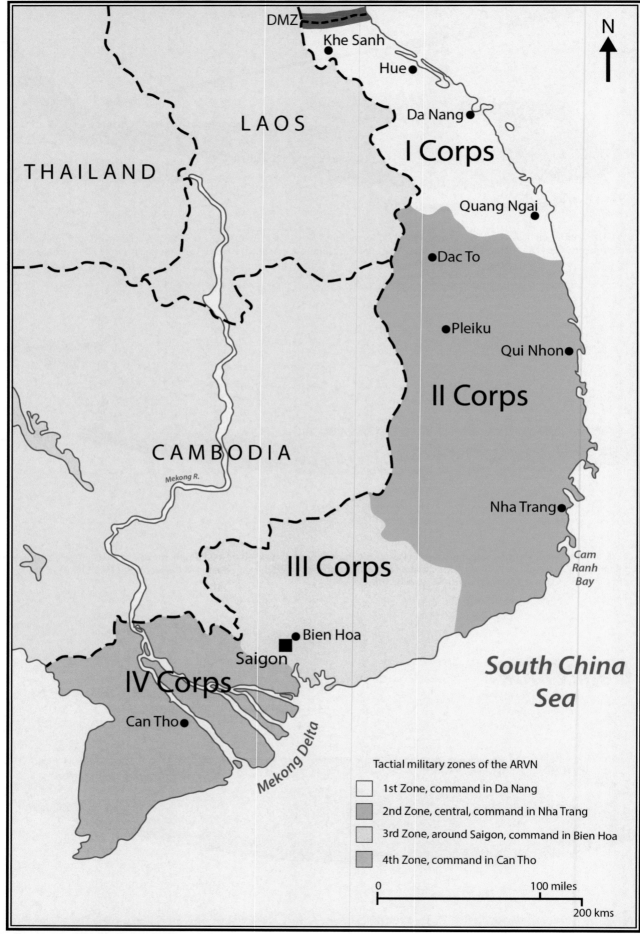

ARVN military zones. (Map by George Anderson)

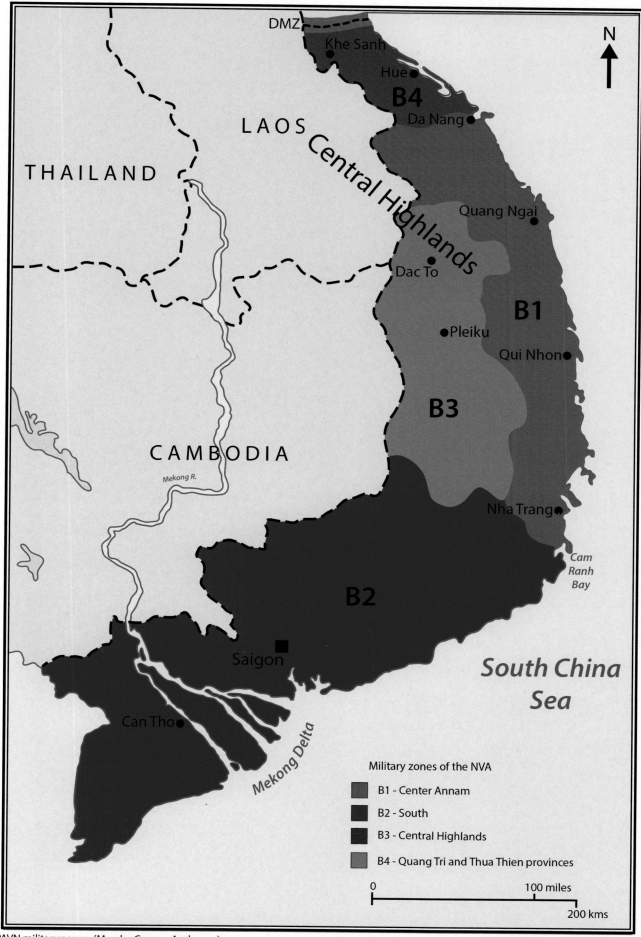

NVA/PAVN military zones. (Map by George Anderson)

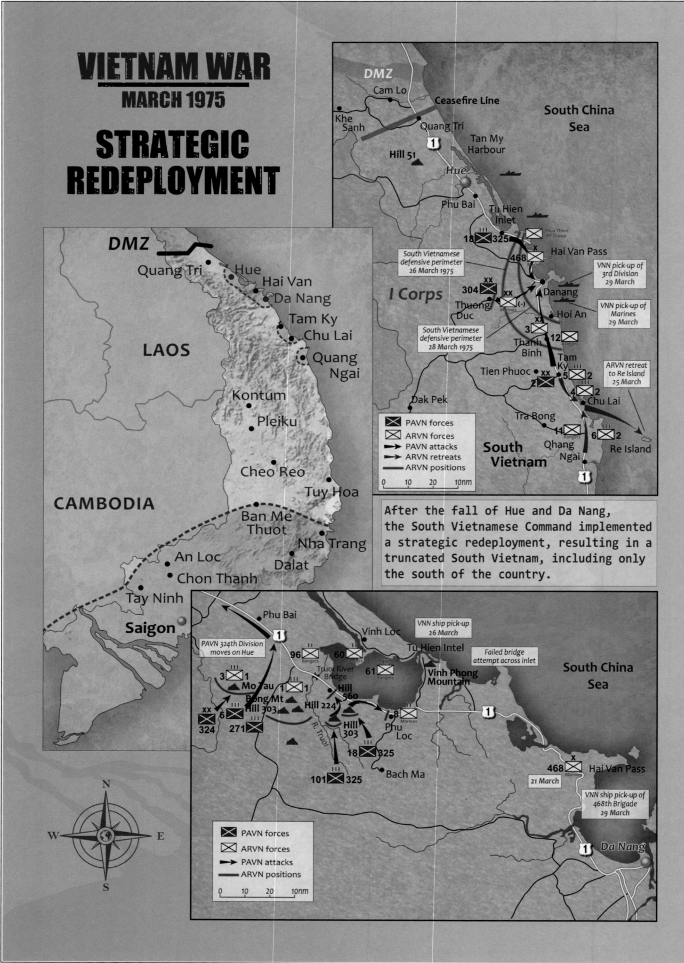

VIETNAM WAR
MARCH 1975
STRATEGIC REDEPLOYMENT

After the fall of Hue and Da Nang, the South Vietnamese Command implemented a strategic redeployment, resulting in a truncated South Vietnam, including only the south of the country.

(Map by Anderson Subtil)

the 11th Ranger Group, and the Quang Ngai Regional Forces, after suffering a two-hour artillery barrage pulled back to the city's western defensive line. By midday, the North Vietnamese T-54s reached the outskirts of the town. Now the provincial governor requested an evacuation of the city for a withdrawal towards Chu Lai. Truong approved the request. The South Vietnamese pulled back by blowing up the bridge at Ke Xuyen. It took the PAVN engineers several hours to build a pontoon bridge, allowing the resumption of the attack by the 52nd Brigade, supported by the 3rd Armoured Battalion. At 11:30 p.m. on 24 March, the PAVN was in full control of Quang Ngai.

In the meantime, North Vietnamese intelligence had intercepted a radio message indicating that ARVN forces were retreating towards Chu Lai. The tanks of the 574th Armoured Regiment were redirected and speeded up, trying to catch a retreating ARVN column of over 200 trucks. The T-34/85s and T-54s however had to reduce a series of strong points manned by the 11th Ranger Group that tried to delay the North Vietnamese advance. The North Vietnamese tankers finally caught up with the convoy, when it was ambushed by the PAVN 94th Regiment, almost destroying it. On 25 March, the North Vietnamese tankers resumed their march north along Route

Simultaneously with the capture of Chu Lai airbase, the PAVN 52nd Brigade captured Quang Ngai City. These North Vietnamese troops are deploying an 82mm mortar. (PAVN)

A T-34/85 of the 574th Armoured Regiment entered the Chu Lai airbase on 25 March. All remaining ARVN positions south of Da Nang were captured in five days. (PAVN)

1, opening the route for the 38th Regiment that captured the Ba Ren Bridge but it was soon after destroyed by an air strike, temporarily halting the advance towards Da Nang's southern sector.

Taking profit of this temporary lull, Brigadier General Nhut spent the night of 24 March in his helicopter overseeing the retreating convoys from Quang Ngai City. They reached Chu Lai on the morning but found the place already overcrowded with RF and PF troops and countless refugees. He swarmed in low with his helicopter and with a bullhorn warned the troops to return to their units and take up defensive positions against a possible enemy attack, but it seemed that no one was listening. Nhut then landed on the LST *Nha Trang* (HQ-505) anchored in the bay and with its captain planned the evacuation of the 2nd Division's survivors to Re Island instead of the already overcrowded Da Nang enclave. While Chu Lai had a large pier that could accommodate the ship, the dock

was packed with an unruly mob of approximately 10,000 people. It was then decided to put the LST ashore that night on a nearby beach to pick up his troops. He quickly gathered his staff and commanders to plan the evacuation. All the heavy equipment, the artillery, as well as the ammunition and fuel stocks would be destroyed. To assist with the evacuation, the Navy ordered the LST *Vinh Long* (HQ-802) and the smaller Landing Ship Medium (LSM) *Huong Giang* (HQ-404), plus six small landing craft from Qui Nhon, to divert to Chu Lai. At 9:00 p.m. on 25 March, the LST *Nha Trang* moved to the beach, where about 5,000 soldiers and some M113s had gathered. Once again, the water was too shallow, and the ship went aground 100m offshore. This caused a repeat of the chaotic scenes on the beach near Tu Hien. The discipline soon broke down as the troops rushed to board it. The overloaded M113s drove recklessly into the surf, ramming each other in the struggle to reach the ship and the captain backed away from the beach. Nhut ordered the ship to dock at the pier.

To prevent the mob from storming the ship, it halted 10m from the dock and erected a makeshift gangplank between the pier and the ship. This forced the people to load single file, which greatly reduced the hysteria. At around 1:00 a.m. on 26 March, the other ships arrived at Chu Lai harbour. With the tide running out, only the *Huong Giang* could enter. It tied behind the *Nha Trang* and also took on people. By noon, the majority of the people were loaded, and the ships left the harbour. They attempted to return that night to pick up the 6th Regiment, which was serving as rear guard, but they were unable to enter the harbour because of enemy fire from the banks. The VNN eventually evacuated 10,500 troops and civilians. Some 4,000 were from the 2nd Division, 4,000 from RF units of Quang Tin and Quang Ngai provinces, and the rest were policemen, dependents, and civilians. On 27 March, 6,000 servicemen and dependents disembarked at Re Island, and the rest were, in the end, shipped to Da Nang.

The stunning debacle in I Corps' southern sector, where a whole ARVN division and two Ranger groups were defeated in two days was due more to a collapse of morale than the pressure of the enemy. Indeed, President Thieu's decision to abandon entire provinces caused a panic that spread among the local population around Quang Tri and Hue.

Meanwhile, on the afternoon of 24 March, the Politburo in Hanoi hurriedly met in response to the swiftly changing battlefield in the ARVN I Corps. It had planned to gather on 25 March, but the collapsing Hue pocket and the capture of Tan Ky and Quang Ngai caused it to reconvene sooner. After the PAVN deputy chief of staff, Lieutenant General Le Tron Tan, summarised the military situation, Le Duan intervened. Clearly, he claimed, the South Vietnamese were reeling. With Da Nang teetering on collapse and the ARVN retreating from the Central Highlands, the PAVN needed to step up its attack. The Politburo decided to rapidly assault Da Nang while preparing to conquer Saigon. The next day, the Politburo concluded that the long-heralded "strategic opportunity" had finally arrived. It then outlined the following major decisions. First, Lieutenant General Le Tron Tan was assigned as the overall commander of the PAVN forces in the campaign to conquer Da Nang. Second, the 3rd Strategic Army Corps (SAC) was formed from the separate units in the B3 Front in the Central Highlands. After a time of reshuffling, it would drive down south to join forces with those of the B2 Front to assault Saigon. Third, Le Duc Tho, the North Vietnamese representative that signed the Paris "peace accord" and who had received the Nobel Peace Prize with Henry Kissinger, would go south and meet with Senior General Van Tien Dung, the PAVN Commander in Chief, to explain the Politburo's reasoning. He would then proceed to COSVN (Central Office for South Vietnam) to oversee the assault on Saigon. Most important, the Politburo once again advanced its timetable for liberating South Vietnam. The original plan had called for 1976, with a possible extension into 1977. Then, after the liberation of Ban Me Thuot in the Central Highlands, the date was changed to late 1975. Now, with the imminent destruction of the ARVN I and II Corps, the Politburo decided to conquer Saigon in May, before the onset of the rainy season.

On 26 March, just before departing for the South, Lieutenant General Le Tron Tan met with Giap to discuss his plan to take Da Nang. He initially planned to take five days to reorganise the forces of the B4 and B1 Fronts as well as those of the 2nd SAC before attacking. However, fearing that the enemy would also evacuate this last enclave, Giap ordered him to speed up his preparations and to toss caution aside and advanced without careful planning, with an "attack on the march" strategy. Tan agreed and immediately departed for Da Nang. He had to coordinate the combined forces within a new tactical command organisation, the newly set up Front 475. General Tan envisaged two options: if the enemy succeeded in regrouping and consolidated in Da Nang enclave, then he was prepared to engage in a major battle, engaging not only the theatres' forces, but also bolstered by the 1st SAC that could be diverted there if required. His other proposal was to accelerate the current plan developed by Major General Nguyen Huu An, by putting off balance the retreating ARVN units, trouncing them and not allowing them to regroup and retrench into solid positions. By temperament, Tan favoured that last option. Contrary to the current PAVN practice of rather strictly adhering to well-rehearsed plans, giving little autonomy to local commanders, he instead encouraged them to be bold and take initiative in relation to the battlefield developments. That truly cultural revolution within the highly centralised and disciplined PAVN chains of command would be the trademark of the new North Vietnamese operational art during that last phase of the conflict. The armoured units would lead the attacks, capturing the crossroads and bridges, sowing confusion among the retreating ARVN columns.

The new PAVN strategy surprised Truong who was still relying on previous past experience while fighting the North Vietnamese. He expected that he would have three to four weeks before a new Communist assault. In the past, that was usually the time necessary for them to regroup, replenish and move their troops to their attack positions. But Truong was wrong and did not fully realise the extent of the newly built road networks that the enemy had developed on its western flank, allowing it to shift entire divisions within a week. On 26 March, he then hastily reorganised what was left of his units, about 75,000 soldiers, and deployed them into two successive defensive lines.

On the outer defensive line: The 258th Marine Brigade and the 914th RF Group were to hold all areas between Phuoc Tuong and Lien Chieu. The 369th Marine Brigade and the 57th Regiment, 3rd Division, were to protect Dai Loc and Dong Lam. The surviving elements of the 147th Marine Brigade and the Marine Division Headquarters would hold Nuoc Man (Marble Mountain) airfield. Meanwhile, the remnants of the 3rd Division would hold Vinh Dien and Ninh Que, while the 15th Ranger Group held Ba Ren.

On the inner defensive line: The 912th RF Group, and the last elements of the 11th ACR and 20th Tank Squadron held the Phuoc Tuong – Hoa My sector. The last three battalions of the 1st Division that escaped from Hue, the remaining troops of the evacuated 2nd Division, the 12th Ranger Group, and about 3,000 freshly trained soldiers from the Hoa Cam Training Camp were ordered to defend all key areas between Hoa Cam and Nuoc Man. All independent Regional and Popular Force battalions were placed in reserve and could go into combat when required. There were also 12 artillery battalions at his disposal, as well as the 1st Air Force Division. However, Truong had in the end to comply with the order that he would ultimately retrieve the Marine Division to return it to the ARVN central reserve. In fact, first deprived of the paratroopers, then of the Marines, Truong knew that his chances to hold Da Nang was minimal.

Further compounding his problem was the deteriorating situation on the refugee's front. Da Nang's streets were now overcrowded by 1.5 million refugees fleeing their villages and towns when the ARVN pulled out. On 24 March, the South Vietnamese government

On 25 March 1975, the United States authorised the US Navy Military Sealift Command to dispatch 10 ships to Da Nang to evacuate refugees to the areas still held by the South Vietnamese. One of the most involved was the *Pioneer Contender*, responsible for evacuating an amazing 16,600 refugees by the time Da Nang fell. (US Navy)

had sought international help for managing the massive refugees problem unfolding in its northern abandoned provinces. The United States was specifically asked to send ships to help to evacuate the stranded refugees in the various enclaves along the coast to the South. But Washington was reluctant to be involved and approached its Asian allies to find a solution. Finally, both South Korea and Taiwan agreed to each send two LSTs of their own navies to help. But, as the hours passed by, the situation in Da Nang turned to chaos, with riots breaking out near the food distribution points, while ARVN stragglers and deserters began looting stores, and engaged in gun battles with the local police. As the VNN was mainly engaged in troop

By 27 March, the United States chartered World Airways to use its Boeing 727s to speed up the evacuation of refugees from Da Nang. However, the air bridge was soon shelved when the situation at the airport became out of control. (VNA)

repatriation, the Navy commander stated that he could evacuate no more than 60,000 refugees per month. The government then decided to requisition civilian ships for the assignment but even that measure could not cope with the huge task at hand. President Ford finally overruled the State Department's reservations as well as a hostile Congress and decided, on 25 March, for humanitarian reasons to divert 10 ships of the US Navy Military Sealift Command based in the Philippines towards Da Nang to pick up refugees.

The next day, Truong send his deputy, Major General Hoang Van Lac, to Saigon and pleaded for urgent transportation before the ships could arrive. The Americans then arranged for flights to Da Nang, starting the same day, with aircraft from World Airways. This company based in Oakland, California, had already been operating out of Saigon for several weeks, airlifting rice and ammunition to Phnom Penh, the beleaguered capital of Cambodia, and had a long

history of chartered contracts to fly US troops and supplies around South Vietnam. The first contract was for 20 flights to remove a first batch of refugees from Da Nang airport. The Boeing 727s of World Airways immediately swung into action, taking out 2,000 persons by the evening. The purpose was to evacuate at least 14,000 people in daily runs between Da Nang and Cam Ranh Bay. At the same time, the Americans also shifted six tugs and five barges that had been engaged in the Mekong River convoys hauling supplies to Cambodia to assist in the evacuation. However, on 27 March, when people learned that an ongoing air bridge had been put in place by World Airways, an unruly crowd invaded Da Nang airport in a mad rush to board any available aircraft. By the afternoon a last Boeing 727 took off after the crew had literally to fight off people trying to climb onto it. Afterwards, the field was closed to civilian traffic, but the chaos also disrupted the VNAF air operations. Unable to coordinate its efforts

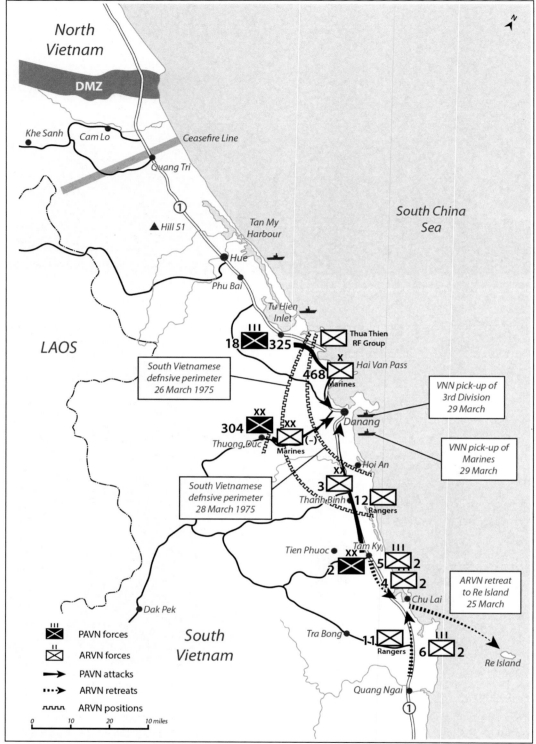

Fall of I Corps. (Map by Tom Cooper)

Map labels:
North Vietnam
DMZ
Khe Sanh
Cam Lo
Ceasefire Line
Quang Tri
(1)
Hill 51
Tan My Harbour
Hue
Phu Bai
Tu Hien Inlet
LAOS
18 ⊠ 325
Thua Thien RF Group
South Vietnamese defnsive perimeter 26 March 1975
468
Hai Van Pass
Marines
304 ⊠
XX
(-)
Thuong Duc
Marines
Danang
VNN pick-up of 3rd Division 29 March
VNN pick-up of Marines 29 March
South China Sea
Hoi An
3 ⊠
XX
South Vietnamese defnsive perimeter 28 March 1975
Thanh Binh 12 ⊠ Rangers
Tam Ky
Tien Phuoc
5 ⊠ 2
2 ⊠ XX
4 ⊠ 2
ARVN retreat to Re Island 25 March
Chu Lai
Dak Pek
South Vietnam
Tra Bong
1-1 ⊠ Rangers
6 ⊠ 2
Re Island
Quang Ngai
(1)

Legend:
PAVN forces
ARVN forces
PAVN attacks
ARVN retreats
ARVN positions
0   10   20   10 miles

equipped respectively with F-5As and F-5Es. Excepting two F-5As and one F-5E that were in maintenance, the two squadrons flew out on 27 March. The 538th Squadron departed though with a "last bang". The F-5Es were fully bombed up and flew a BOBS attack against the North Vietnamese positions west of Da Nang. After releasing their bombs through the overcast, they flew south.

Lieutenant General Le Tron Tan of Front 475 established his attack plan against the Da Nang enclave along four directions. Against the northern perimeter, the 2nd SAC would capture the Hai Van Pass, then its 325th Division (without the 95th Regiment), with support from one tank battalion and one artillery battalion, were ordered to advance along Highway 1 and capture the ARVN I Corps headquarters, the 1st Air Force Division Headquarters, and then move on to the Son Tra Peninsula to capture the main seaport there. In the northwest sector, the 9th Regiment, 304th Division, with support from one tank battalion, one artillery battalion and one anti-aircraft gun battalion, were ordered to advance along Highway 14B, and capture the ARVN 3rd Division Headquarters at Phuoc Tuong, and then move on to Da Nang Air Base. On the south and southeast perimeters, the 2nd Division, with support of the 36th Artillery Regiment, one artillery battalion, one tank battalion, one anti-aircraft gun battalion, and one anti-tank weapons company (AT-3 Sagger missiles), were ordered to take Da Nang Air Base, then capture the city itself. The 3rd and 68th Regiments were placed in reserve. Against the southwest perimeter, the North Vietnamese engaged the 304th Division (less the 9th Regiment) to take over all the positions held by the 369th Marine Brigade along the Thuong Duc-Ai Nghia – Hiep Duc defensive line, then to advance towards the Marble Mountain airfield. The 24th Regiment, 304th Division was required to capture Hoa Cam and then move on to Da Nang. In a second echelon, Tan had at his disposal the 324th Division with the 1st and 2nd Armoured Battalions, 203rd Armoured Brigade, and the 52nd Brigade with the 574th Armoured Regiment. Newly introduced and serving as a

with Truong about the optimum use of his air assets, the VNAF CO, Lieutenant General Tran Van Minh, decided to take things into his own hands. On 26 March, he dispatched his deputy, Major General Vo Xuan Lanh, to Da Nang to assess the situation. He was directed to save as many assets as possible but still maintain a residual force to sustain the Da Nang enclave. Above all, Minh wanted to save his most modern equipment, notably the brand-new F-5Es. There were some arguments against maintaining them at Da Nang since a North Vietnamese air strike now would have devastating effects on the base. Nevertheless, concluding that the situation was very bleak, Minh agreed to evacuate both the 536th and 538th Squadrons, reserve was the 126th Naval Infantry Regiment that could be used to exploit any breakthroughs or for naval disembarking operations.

The main problem for Tan was to speed up the deployment of his tanks and artillery so that they would be positioned in time to support the offensive. The 203rd Armoured Brigade had its four battalions still dispersed between Dong Ha and the Laotian border, while the units that had helped take Hue were redirected towards Da Nang. It took four days for the tanks of the brigade to move some 300km through bad mountain tracks. Some 20 percent of its vehicles were left behind during the trek, many broken down or bogged down. On one occasion, while approaching a South Vietnamese position, it appeared that the road was heavily mined on a stretch of 6km. It took a whole day to remove the mines. Due to the circumstances, by 28 March, the 203rd Armoured Brigade could only deploy 101 tanks and APCs for the final push against Da Nang. It was nevertheless reinforced by a further 60 tanks of the 574th Armoured Regiment in the southern sector and some 20 M48s and T-54s of two companies arriving from Hue.

The heavy artillery unit of the 2nd SAC, the 164th Artillery Regiment with its long-range 122mm, 130mm and 152mm guns, also left Hue to be positioned on the northern fringes of the Da Nang defence perimeter. By the evening of 28 March, a battery of 130mm guns began pounding Da Nang airbase. On the night of 27 March, the 572nd and 575th Artillery Regiments were also within reach of Da Nang's southern perimeter with their heavy guns and MRLs. Tan continuously pressed his corps' rear services to unsnarl any logistics jams and to use ARVN equipment to replace or augment their own. The PAVN columns moved in despite persistent VNAF air strikes, with an average of 33 attack sorties per day, forcing the 2nd SAC's organic air defence asset, the 673rd Anti-Aircraft Artillery Division to redeploy its unit to cover them. The 284th Anti-Aircraft Artillery Regiment was then attached to the 324th Division, the 285th Anti-

Aircraft Artillery Regiment operated with the 325th Division, and the 245th Anti-Aircraft Artillery Regiment with the 304th Division. The 274th Missile Regiment redeployed its batteries of SA-2 (S-75) missiles to cover the northern and western sectors of the North Vietnamese forces facing Da Nang. The southern sector was covered by the 573rd Anti-Aircraft Artillery Regiment as well as two independent battalions with 37mm AA guns.

Taking the Hai Van Pass was of the utmost importance, being the last chokepoint where the PAVN units could be pinned down. General An gave the task to his deputy, Major General Hoang Dan, who had to overcome some major problems. Only the 18th Regiment, 325th Division, was close to the Hai Van Pass. His other units were still in Hue and the bridge on Route 1 over the Truoi River had been destroyed. He told his engineers to rebuild it so that he could resume his advance to the Hai Van Pass. He reinforced the 18th Regiment with the 3rd Armoured Battalion and two batteries of 130mm guns. An himself would join the 304th Division west of Da Nang which was battling for two days to take the ARVN FSB "Baldy". The VNAF reacted vigorously and destroyed several Communist tanks. An ordered the division to be reinforced by the 4th Armoured Battalion before resuming its advance towards Da

By early March, the PAVN's 304th Division, that was still recovering from the heavy losses of the previous year's campaign, was fully operational again after receiving replacement troops. It was now attacking Da Nang's south-western perimeter. Troops moved in on GAZ-63 trucks. (PAVN)

A company of PT-76 tanks of the 3rd Battalion, 203rd Armoured Brigade was assigned to support the PAVN 325th Division to take the strategic Hai Van Pass. (PAVN)

On 28 March 1975, the PAVN 18th Regiment, 325th Division, captured the Hai Van Pass after two days of hard fighting, opening the northern gate of Da Nang. (PAVN)

Trying to stem the 304th Division's advance, the 369th Marine Brigade established a defensive line along the Thuong Duc-Ai Nghia – Hiep Duc sector. The main defence position was anchored on FSB "Baldy" whose 105mm howitzers covered most of Route 14's western approach. (ARVN)

Supporting the 369th Marine Brigade were elements of the ARVN 3rd Division, trying to stop the advance of the PAVN 304th Division. An M41 of the 11th ACS, the organic armoured unit of the division, supported troops at Ky Chau village, some 40km southwest of Da Nang. (ARVN)

Opening the way for the PAVN's 304th Division was this reconnaissance team on a Soviet built IMZ M-72 motorcycle and sidecar. (PAVN)

After taking the Hai Van Pass, the PAVN's 325th Division continued south in its advance along Route 1, spearheaded by the T-54s of the 3rd Battalion, 203rd Armoured Brigade. (PAVN)

Closely following the armoured unts of the PAVN's 203rd Brigade were the fuel bowsers. This fuel cistern version of the ZIL-150 truck is seen refuelling a BTR-50. (PAVN)

Nang along Route 14. A "deep penetration" group was spearheading, constituted by the 9th Regiment and the tanks.

Meanwhile, on 26 March, the 18th Regiment pushed into the northern entrance of the Hai Van Pass but could not advance much, the 458th Marine Brigade beneficing of an excellent air support. On the next morning, Hoang Dan resumed his attack and pushed forward, forcing the Marines to withdraw to not be encircled. Throughout the day, the 18th Regiment engaged RF troops holding positions near the pass. Dan's troops finally pushed through, but then faced another problem: a bridge on Route 1 that had been blown up by PAVN sappers a week earlier. The engineers were unable to repair it in time, so Dan left his heavy armour and artillery behind and moved forward with seven amphibious PT-76 tanks and some APCs. He was himself commanding at the forefront inside a BTR-50. At 5:30 a.m. on 28 March, a battalion of the 18th

An M48 of the ARVN 20th Tank Squadron firing against the approaching North Vietnamese, north of Da Nang. (Nguyen Van Minh Collection)

On 29 March, the PAVN's 304th Division, supported by the T-54s of the 4th Battalion, 203rd Armoured Brigade, reached the western outskirts of Da Nang along Route 14. (PAVN)

Soldiers of the PAVN 304th Division inspecting a knocked out VNMC LVTP-5 amphibious tractor. (PAVN)

For the final assault against Da Nang, the PAVN's 2nd SAC distributed its air defence assets evenly to protect the ground units. This battery of S-60 57mm radar-guided guns belonging to the 284th Anti-Aircraft Artillery Regiment, 675th Anti-Aircraft Artillery Division, overlooked Da Nang Bay and harbour, in support of the arriving 324th Division. (PAVN)

Closely following the advance of the PAVN's 2nd SAC against Da Nang was the 274th SAM Regiment, 675th Anti-Aircraft Artillery Division, with their SA-2 (S-75) missiles. (PAVN)

Da Nang's southern sector was also crumbling, on 28 March, with the renewed attacks of the PAVN's 2nd Division with as a vanguard a "deep penetration" group made up of 31 tanks and a battalion mounted on trucks. On the frontal glacis of this Type 63 light tank was painted the traditional Vietnamese war cry: "Determined to Win". (PAVN)

The PAVN 2nd Division was covered by the 573rd Anti-Aircraft Artillery Regiment, including this 37mm gun. (PAVN)

On 29 March, the PAVN 2nd Division had overcome RF and Ranger resistance near Hoi An and was closing to the Marble Mountain airbase. Still leading were the Type 63s and K-63s of the 574th Armoured Regiment. (PAVN)

Accompanying the PAVN 2nd Division's advance were the 572nd and 575th Artillery Regiments that soon took under their fire Da Nang's logistic centres and airbase. An ATS-59 tractor is seen here towing a D-74 122mm long-range gun. (PAVN)

Concurrently with North Vietnamese guns opening fire on Da Nang's southern perimeter, the PAVN also deployed its artillery against the northern sector. This battery of D-20 152mm guns of the 164th Artillery Regiment was preparing to fire against Da Nang's harbour. (PAVN)

A battery of ARVN M114 155mm howitzers tried to counter-fire the North Vietnamese artillery pounding. (Nguyen Van Minh Collection)

was temporarily halted when the bridges of Cau Lau and Ba Reng were destroyed by VNAF A-37Bs. The North Vietnamese requisitioned canoes and small river craft from the neighbouring fishing villages to ferry the 1st and 31st Regiments across. Only two Type 63 amphibious tanks could cross with them, though a dozen more followed the next morning with a company of K-63 APCs. By midday, the engineers had built two pontoon bridges that allowed the rest of tanks and artillery to continue.

By now, the North Vietnamese artillery had begun pounding Da Nang, particularly targeting the airfield and logistic centres. The pounding also interrupted the US Navy's evacuation of refugees at the harbour where the American ships *Pioneer Contender*, *Sgt. Andrew Miller*, *Pioneer Commander*, and *American Challenger*, had begun their work on the previous day. The ships moved out to sea, but the tugs intended for the Cambodian operations were now arriving and shuttled between the docks and the MSC ships. The ARVN I Corps headquarters was also heavily hit, forcing General Truong to move his command post to the Da Nang naval base. Communication with Saigon was cut, but not before

Regiment, followed by the PT-76s, assaulted the Hai Van Pass. By midday, Lang Co, which also served as an artillery base, was taken and fifteen 105mm howitzers were captured. The North Vietnamese also moved in 30 long-range artillery pieces of the 84th and 164th Artillery Regiments to be positioned at Lang Co, Phuoc Tuong, and Mui Trau. Joined now by the T-54s, the PT-76s drove down the mountain, causing panic among the RF troops. They captured the Thuy Tu Bridge without resistance. The tanks now reached the small port of Song Tra. The T-54s of the 4th Tank Company rolled down the pier, firing against the departing boats.

Meanwhile, the 304th Division continued to face fierce resistance from the ARVN 3rd Division but would resume its advance when the 369th Marine Brigade was ordered to pull back towards Da Nang's inner defence perimeter. On 28 March, its 66th Regiment captured Ai Nghia and had the Marble Mountain airbase under artillery fire. South of Da Nang, the PAVN 2nd Division continued to press on, with as a vanguard a "deep penetration" group made up of 31 tanks and a battalion mounted on trucks. But their advance

the JGS warned him that signal intelligence had now gleaned that the PAVN intended to launch a full-scale assault at 5:00 a.m. the next morning. On the basis of that information, Truong made the decision to abandon the city. That night, he called a meeting with his commanders and told them to move their troops to the beach. The CO of the 3rd Division, Major General Hinh, protested by saying that he could not plan a move with so little time. When Truong said nothing, Hinh realised he had no choice.

The VNN immediately moved to pick up units from the beach. The 468th Marine Brigade was successfully evacuated by the LSM *Lam Giang* (HQ-402) at the foot of the Hai Van Pass at 06:00 a.m. on 29 March. The 369th Marine Brigade retreated to a beach south of Da Nang, between An Dong and My Khe, with the PAVN 304th Division in hot pursuit. The brigade began to board the LSM *Huong Giang* (HQ-404), the same ship that had helped rescue the survivors of the 2nd Division at Chu Lai. Colonel Nguyen Thanh Tri helped Lieutenant General Truong wade out to the ship. As the Marines loaded, PAVN gunners began to shell the beach. The *Huong Giang* was forced to back away after picking up about 500 Marines. When PAVN forces arrived, the Marines resisted for several hours, but eventually 3,000 surrendered. In the 3rd Division sector, only one regiment made it to the landing zone, where HQ-402 picked them up. Only about a thousand troops out of approximately 12,000 made it onto the ship; the rest were stranded.

The VNAF also tried to evacuate the maximum number of people. On the night of 28 March, some eight C-130As landed to retrieve stranded VNAF airmen but the aircraft were swarmed by a mass of refugees and leaderless soldiers. Most of them flew back overloaded, with an average of 200 passengers onboard. In the morning, the A-37Bs continued to fly a series of air strikes covering the western perimeter, destroying several enemy tanks despite intense anti-aircraft fire. However, the ever-increasing shelling of Da Nang AB gravely disrupted subsequent air operations to cover the evacuation of troops by sea. Under fire, civilians took cover inside the aircraft shelters, making the servicing of parked aircraft impossible. In the light of corresponding reports, VNAF General Minh ordered the evacuation of as many operational aircraft as possible. Mechanics tried now to make the stored Caribou of the 427th Transport Squadron flyable again. The unit had been deactivated in November 1974 due to budgetary constraints. At least two C-7s could fly out. Before too long, thousands of people gathered at the air base, attempting to climb on anything offering the hope of escape. Some departing pilots told of seeing a UH-1H on the maintenance ramp fully packed with people waiting for the flight crew, not realising that the helicopter did not have rotor blades. About half of the more than 60 A-37Bs still available

With Da Nang harbour under artillery fire, it was decided on 29 March 1975 to evacuate what remained of the Marine and 3rd Divisions from two landing spots: at the foot of the Hai Van Pass, and the My Khe beach about 6km east of the city. Most of the units gathered at this last location but the VNN ships could not beach and the troops had to wade out to try to climb onboard. (Nguyen Van Minh Collection)

These tankers of the 20th Tank Squadron, I Armoured Brigade, had also driven their M48 tanks to My Khe hoping to be picked up by a ship. (Nguyen Van Minh Collection)

These ARVN M113s tried to swim out to sea to try to catch a VNN ship. Ironically, it was at My Khe, also known by the Americans as "China Beach", that the US Marines landed 10 years earlier beginning direct US involvement in the Vietnam War. (Nguyen Van Minh Collection)

had been evacuated, most of these making final bombing sorties before recovering at Phan Rang for refuelling and continuing towards Bien Hoa or Tan Son Nhut, around Saigon.

Suddenly, during a lull in the artillery barrage, a lone World Airways Boeing 727 appeared and landed with a team of foreign TV journalists onboard. Two M113 APCs escorted the airliner to the parking area. A huge crowd surged forward when it stopped. In a shameful scramble, hundreds of desperate soldiers fought their way through the refugees and began to climb aboard. The aircraft's captain moved forward while dozens were still clinging to the rear door. While accelerating along the runway, the airliner was pursued by countless cars and motorcycles. Worse yet, several soldiers who were clinging to the landing gear were crushed to death when this was retracted. Landing back at Saigon, the crew counted 330 passengers on board. Amid enemy shells exploding, the pilot of an AC-119K gunship of the 821st Attack Squadron later reported that he had to taxi over 100 dead bodies on the ramp before he could make it to the runway.

The helicopters and observation aircraft lacked the range to escape south since many of the air bases on their route were already in

On 29 March, the PAVN 2nd Division reached the southern suburbs of Da Nang. These inhabitants welcomed them by waving traditional Buddhist flags in sign of peace and neutrality. The massacres carried out by the Communists during the 1968 Tet Offensive at Hue were still vividly remembered. (Nguyen Van Minh Collection)

The appearance of the North Vietnamese tanks surprised the last VNAF pilots trying to take off. This A-37B, fully loaded for a close air support mission with two M117 750lb, four Mk 82 500lb, and two Mk 81 250lb bombs, was damaged by hits on its left wing. The pilot veered it off the runway before being caught by the tankers. (PAVN

Communist hands. Consequently, many helicopter pilots flew their machines to the pick-up point at the end of the Hai Van Pass or at the foot of the Marble Mountain, hoping to embark on a ship. Others flew to Cu Re Island, some 40km west of Chu Lai. The island served as a base for Air America, the Central Intelligence Agency-owned "airline", and as a regrouping point for the ARVN before their transhipment towards the south. Dozens of other helicopters took their chance anyway, pressing south as far as possible before landing in enemy-controlled areas. Other choose to ditch at sea, hoping to be rescued by passing ships. The crews of the 213rd and 239th Helicopter Squadrons apparently attempted a concerted evacuation plan on the night of 28 March. About half of their Hueys took off and pressed on south in very bad weather. Less than a quarter of them succeeded in reaching Phu Cat AB a few hours before this was also overrun. Many surviving pilots reported hearing radio messages from wingmen announcing that they were out of fuel and forced to land in the areas controlled by the North Vietnamese. One crew was

The "penetration group" of the PAVN 2nd Division reached Da Nang airbase at midday of 29 March. Infantry advanced cautiously towards one of the gates under the protection of Type 63 tank of the 574th Armoured Regiment. (PAVN)

Among the aircraft captured at Da Nang AB were the mothballed Cessna O-2As of the 110th Observation Squadron. The unit had been also deactivated for budgetary saving measures. (PAVN)

The North Vietnamese captured 169 aircraft at Da Nang AB, including these mothballed C-7B Caribous of the 427th Transport Squadron. The unit had been deactivated in November 1974 for budgetary reasons. (PAVN)

The first F-5E captured by the North Vietnamese was this one from the 538th Fighter Squadron. It could not be evacuated, being in maintenance. (PAVN)

Without directives, with the Corps commander out of contact, military discipline collapsed, and the remaining ARVN troops melted away. Some 6,000 men of the 2nd Division laid down their arms. The 3,000 new recruits at the Hoa Cam training centre also surrendered. But others continued to resist desperately, particularly in the southern sector, along Route 1 and continued to slow down the advance of the PAVN 2nd Division, forcing its lead regiment to keep stopping to engage RF troops. After the third incident, the division commander sacked the regimental commander for not bypassing the defenders. By the end of the morning, the tanks of the 574th Armoured Regiment reached the outskirt of the Da Nang AB. When the T-54s and Type 63s broke through to the base, a group of A-37Bs were taking off. The tanks engaged them with their guns and machineguns and one damaged fighter-bomber, fully loaded with bombs, veered off the runway before stopping, the pilot being taken as prisoner. A group of 12 C-130As then appeared overhead intending to pick up the last survivors. Seeing tanks on the runways, they flew back to Saigon.

The PAVN 325th Division had meanwhile secured Lien Chieu, the Nam O Bridge and the Trinh Me The Bridge, thereby clearing the main road for the supporting tank and armoured units to advance on Son Tra where the last troops of the ARVN 3rd Division had dug in. On the afternoon of 29 March, North Vietnamese soldiers of the 2nd, 304th, 324th and 325th Divisions, as well as the 574th Armoured Regiment and the 203rd Armoured Brigade, entered the city of Da Nang. The next morning, some 168 tanks and APCs were mustered, supported by artillery and MRLs, to move to Son Tra for final mop up operations.

even heard saying a goodbye to everybody before choosing to crash at sea, killing themselves, rather being captured by the Communists.

The T-54s of the 3rd Battalion, 203rd Armoured Brigade, supporting the PAVN 325th Division also entered into Da Nang from the north. Due to the lack of APCs, North Vietnamese infantry often rode atop the tanks. (PAVN

The troops of the PAVN 325th Division found this M151 jeep abandoned in a street in Da Nang. It was armed with an M40 106mm recoilless rifle in an anti-tank configuration. (PAVN)

The PAVN 304th Division also reached downtown Da Nang by the rainy afternoon of 29 March 1975, with the T-54s of the 4th Battalion, 203rd Armoured Brigade, leading. (PAVN)

This intact M107 175mm SP gun was found abandoned in a street in Da Nang. (PAVN)

The North Vietnamese captured much American built equipment. Always lacking in APCs, they happily put into service any serviceable M113. (PAVN)

The PAVN captured a lot of armour of the ARVN I Armoured Brigade in Da Nang. That included these M48 tanks as well as M88 and M578 recovery vehicles. (PAVN)

In the meantime, after being evacuated from Chu Lai to Re Island, the remnants of the ARVN 2nd Division had lost contact with I Corps Headquarters and had been stranded on the island. Fortunately for the troops, on 1 April, one of the engines of LST *Da Nang* (HQ-501) broke down as it was sailing south. An alert soldier spotted the ship when it hove-to off the island to make repairs. Brigadier General Tran Van Nhut, CO of the 2nd Division, flew his personal helicopter out to the HQ-501. After a short discussion, the LST captain agreed to transport Nhut's troops to Cam Ranh Bay. Enroute, Nhut received orders to divert to Ham Tan instead, further down the coast, between Phan Rang and Phan Thiet. These would be the last ARVN troops retrieved from the I Corps.

According to North Vietnamese figures for the entire campaign against the ARVN I Corps, from 5 to 29 March, PAVN forces eliminated almost 120,000 enemy troops from the field of battle, with only 16,000 who managed to escape. Of this total, 55,000 were captured on the battlefield, while the rest deserted their units and

turned themselves in. The Communists captured for their own use 179 tanks and APCs, 327 artillery pieces, 47 ships and boats, 1,084 military vehicles. There were also 169 aircraft, out of this total the VNAF had time to sabotage and destroy 40 airframes. The North Vietnamese captured 29 A-37Bs, two F-5As, and one F-5E that the VPAF tried to make operational again. The total VNAF losses during the final campaign in the Da Nang area amounted to some 268 aircraft, valued at $106 million, written off as of 4 April due to all causes. Furthermore, the Air Force lost $48 million worth of ammunition.

The television images of Da Nang's panicky and very public collapse seemed to confirm long-held impressions in the West that the ARVN was a house of cards waiting for the first strong gust to blow it over. While the panic displayed at the evacuation points was a disgrace, for the most part South Vietnamese forces had fought well, however. It was not until late in the campaign that numerous factors caused a sudden and irreversible breakdown of morale. The decision

Found abandoned at the northern entry of Da Nang along Route 1 was this group of ARVN vehicles. It included M48 tanks, an M113 APC, an M151 jeep and M35 trucks. The PAVN vehicle driving away is a BJ-212 "Beijing" command car. (PAVN)

PAVN troops inspecting captured ARVN M113s in Da Nang. Many of them were quickly put into service with the North Vietnamese armoured unit driving towards Saigon. (PAVN)

Captured at the Da Nang harbour was this V100 armoured car. Unusually, a .50-cal machine gun had been added at the front of the vehicle. Note also the abandoned VNAF UH-1H helicopter in the background. (PAVN)

The North Vietnamese also captured this BGM-71 TOW anti-missile launcher. This anti-tank system was introduced into ARVN service from 1972. (PAVN)

of President Thieu to abandon nearly 80 percent of the I Corps area to the enemy caused confusion and incomprehension. Later, General Truong reported that the most significant problem facing him were the hundreds of thousands of refugees who moved in an uncontrollable mass into Hue and Da Nang. This force represented for him a greater danger and contributed more to the defeat of the ARVN than did the enemy. Combat units attempting to deploy were swallowed up in the mass of humanity, then spread confusion and panic to them. If Thieu gambled by wanting to dramatize the situation by pulling out of some areas in the northern part of the country, hoping that Washington would react and resume military aid, he lost. Nothing now could stop the North Vietnamese from converging on Saigon.

6

THE ARVN REORGANISES

While Da Nang was falling, the North Vietnamese forces that had taken the Central Highlands continued attacking down the coast, overwhelming all attempted resistance to protect the ports of Nha Trang and Cam Ranh as described in *Target Saigon Volume 2*. That last location was initially chosen to disembark the refugees arriving from Da Nang. It was also there that, on 20 March, the 3rd Airborne Brigade, taken out of I Corps, was also disembarked to take a blocking position on the M'Drak Pass on Route 21, trying to stop the North Vietnamese forces attacking from Ban Me Thout. On 1 April, the American MSC ships loaded with refugees in Da Nang arrived at Cam Ranh Bay. The place was supposed to be a safe haven for them. Although the captain of the *Pioneer Commander* repeatedly radioed MSC headquarters about a band of thugs who were terrorising the people on the ship, no one in Saigon alerted the South Vietnamese military at Cam Ranh. When the ship docked, the thugs disembarked and slipped away and easily overwhelmed the guard force of the ARVN 5th Logistic Centre and shot and seriously wounded its commander who tried to stop them from stealing his vehicles. Another MSC ship, *Sgt. Andrew Miller* docked empty and picked the refugees back up in an orderly fashion the next day. The

next ship that arrived, the *Greenville Victory*, was overwhelmed by a mass of refugees and decided to pull back and the captain decided to use a barge to ferry people to the ship. In the panic, many were crushed against the pier or between the barge and the ship or drowned. The ship finally departed after loading 9,000 people. The following ship, the *American Challenger*, would also load until dawn in chaotic conditions.

Meanwhile, on 30 March, the fleet that had evacuated the troops from Da Nang, mostly Marines, also dropped anchor in Cam Ranh Bay. The commander of II Corps, Major General Pham Van Phu, went to see the CO of I Corps, Lieutenant General Ngo Quang Truong, who had just arrived in the port. Truong had been Phu's boss in 1972 when Phu commanded the 1st Division around Hue. Phu wanted Truong to release the Marines, but Truong refused to speak to him. The main reason was Truon's anger at Phu for the disastrous retreat from the Central Highlands, which had helped destroy I Corps.

It was Truong's strangest action of the war, for without the Marines, Phu had no chance. Truong was however depressed and in poor physical condition, requiring intravenous injections. He

One of the main tasks for ARVN was regrouping, processing, and reorganising the remnants of the units evacuated from the abandoned northern provinces. These Marines are disembarking at Vung Tau, some 130km southeast of Saigon, from VNN frigates that had picked them up at Da Nang. (ARVN)

also appeared dejected and in poor morale due to the loss of the I Corps. When the JGS ordered the Marines to disembark at Cam Ranh and told Truong to return to Saigon alone, he refused. He told the ship's captain to call the General Staff to ask that the Marines be allowed to return to Saigon along with him for a rest. If this request was refused, he would remain in Cam Ranh with the Marines and would fight at their side. Truong probably feared that if he returned alone, President Thieu would arrest him for the loss of the I Corps, and wanted to stay with the Marines because they provided him protection. The JGS quickly rescinded the order and ordered the two depleted Marine brigades to go back to the ships and returned to Vung Tau, near Saigon. On 3 April, the North Vietnamese tanks rolled into Cam Ranh.

The incident illustrated well the fragmented and divided ARVN high command. Already, the pull-out of the Airborne Division, even if it was a rational tactical choice, was also interpreted by some as a measure by Thieu to bring back this praetorian guard unit to protect his regime inside the capital. In fact, Thieu was now facing an increasing political opposition, worsened by the defeats suffered in the northern provinces. The Catholics, traditional supporters of the regime, now organised a wide demonstration campaign in the main cities, led by the redemptorist priest Tran Huu Thanh, against the alleged corruption of some close associates with Thieu with his People's Anti-Corruption Movement. They were joined by the trade unions and journalists, as well as some congressmen who went on a symbolic hunger strike inside the parliament. Important moderate opposition figures like Tran Van Do or Bui Diem who at first called for a wider government including them were also now opposed to Thieu. Part of the parliamentary opposition also tried to rally Truong Vinh Le, a former president of the Lower House during the presidency of Ngo Dinh Diem, within the new National Progressive Party. There was also opposition from some Buddhists, as well as the Hoa Hao and Cao Dai religious sects. Thieu tightened the control

regime on the South Vietnamese press, accusing it of instilling fear and anger among public opinion by describing the ordeal of the refugees in the evacuated areas. He also ordered a crackdown in early April against supposed plotters who were preparing a coup. Among the arrested was Nguyen Van Ngan, a former minister and an important figure of the Democracy Party, the party created by Thieu, and which had the majority of the seats in the Lower House. Ten high-ranking politicians of the Action Committee, close to former Premier and Vice President, Vice Air Marshal Nguyen Cao Ky, were also arrested. Ky, a northerner who came south after the partition of the country in 1954, had long been viewed by Thieu with suspicion, with his extensive support within the VNAF, the National Police and political parties close to the northern refugees. Despite the ongoing repressive measures taken against his political opponents, the Senate defiantly voted for a resolution seeking the resignation of Thieu. The President of the Senate and former Foreign Affairs Minister who signed the Peace Accords in Paris in 1973 for South Vietnam, Tran Van Lam, also asked Thieu to resign. Lam's intent was to form a national-unity government, with Ky as head of the council that could negotiate an accommodation with Hanoi or a coalition with the Provisional Revolutionary Government. But Thieu reacted abusively, accusing his former supporter of having deserted him. He refused to consider either resigning or handing over real power to a new government.

In reality, Thieu did not care about the political opposition. He did not believe that Hanoi would negotiate with a government headed by Lam or Ky, given that the North Vietnamese now had the upper hand on the battlefield. Even if Hanoi continued to speak of a political solution, by suggesting that an accommodation would be possible with the "Neutralist Third Force", around former General Duong Van Minh with the left-wing Catholics and the Buddhists of the An Quang Temple, that was only to sow division among the Saigon regime. By exploiting Thieu's image as an uncompromising hawk while playing on South Vietnamese fears of American abandonment, the Politburo hoped to unravel Saigon's command structure in order to ease the conquest.

More than these civil disturbances, Thieu feared the most that his military would put the blame for the debacle in the northern provinces on his "redeployment strategy". He acted first and decided to punish the "cowards and defeatists" as announced during a television speech. That would be translated into the arrest of several high-ranking officers that had recently failed on the battlefield, including Major General Pham Van Phu and Lieutenant General Lam Quang Thi for the debacle in II Corps and I Corps Forward respectively. Two other generals were Pham Quoc Thuan and Du Quoc Dong, blamed for the fall of Phuoc Long in January

An ARVN processing centre near Vung Tau inventorying the rifles of evacuated troops to redistribute them to newly reorganised units. (ARVN)

1975. Lieutenant General Ngo Quang Truong, CO of I Corps and Brigadier General Bui The Lan, CO of the Marine Division, were spared. They loudly voiced their disapproval of these arrests, arguing that these men were victims of an injustice, being far more competent than Thieu's loyalists in Saigon. Their prosecution would probably fracture the ARVN more, being widely respected as being among the most able tacticians of the South Vietnamese armed forces. Although most civilian leaders were calling for his head, and there was much badmouthing in the military, Thieu retained the loyalty of the senior military officers. General Cao Van Vien, the chief of the General Staff, Lieutenant General Nguyen Van Toan, CO of III Corps around Saigon, and even the Air Force commander, Lieutenant General Tran Van Minh, continued to back him. Thieu needed a scapegoat for the recent defeats and fired the Prime Minister Tran Thien Khiem on 4 April, as well as the entire cabinet. Concurrently, Thieu nominated as new Prime Minister the Speaker of the House, Nguyen Ba Can, at the head of a new "fighting government devoted to fight the enemy and defeatism". As he had done so often in the past, Thieu had outmanoeuvred his domestic opponents. Still, his hold on power depended entirely upon continued American support and, just as important, upon reversing the military tide.

A group of South Vietnamese congressmen protested in front of the National Assembly. They asked the dismissal of President Nguyen Van Thieu after the disastrous evacuations of the northern provinces. (Albert Grandolini Collection)

Students demonstrated against the riot control police in Saigon in March 1975. They protested against the lowering of the draft age into the Army to 17 years old. (Nguyen Van Minh Collection)

But on this issue, the things were bleaker than ever. Since the fall of Phuoc Long in January 1975 and which marked the beginning of the final North Vietnamese campaign against South Vietnam, President Ford tried his best to overcome a hostile Congress and US public opinion to increase aid to Saigon. Several schemes were envisaged by the Washington Special Action Group (WSAG), a National Security Council committee designed to handle serious crises and make policies and contingency plans. The new United States President appeared very weak on the domestic scene, having succeeded Richard Nixon in August 1974 after the Watergate Scandal. He resigned himself to not send troops back into Vietnam, a fact confirmed in a TV news conference on 21 January, when he admitted he could not foresee any circumstances in which American forces might return. He also knew that the aid request

had little chance of success, but he would not abandon the fight. He was persuaded that the situation could be saved if the United States resumed their aid at the adequate level allowed by the Paris Accords. To win over Congress, he offered to limit aid for a single three-year package, provided Congress granted an adequate amount. He proposed that Congress send a bi-partisan group to travel to South Vietnam and to provide testimony to the various committees. The Congress delegation indeed visited South Vietnam from 25 February to 3 March, led by John Flynt, a supporter of continued aid to South Vietnam and included Bella Abzug, Donald M. Frazer, and Peter McCloskey, all opponents of continued aid. They returned to Washington when the North Vietnamese were preparing to attack the Central Highlands. The delegation was unable to reach a unified position and postponed a vote on the matter. Meanwhile, while the situation on the ground deteriorated at great speed, President Thieu dispatched Nguyen Tieng Hung, his special envoy, to Washington, together with a delegation of the South Vietnamese Congress. Hung brought with him several secret letters from former President Nixon, personally addressed to Thieu, and containing promises of air support in case of "Communist blatant violation of the cease-fire". But Saigon's delegation found mostly closed doors. Worse, the revelation of the letters only created a new scandal, many in the US Congress found in them the duplicity of Nixon about his handling of the South-East Asian affairs and the delegation returned to Saigon empty handed. Whatever Thieu's real motives might have been, his last trump cards brought no positive reply from Washington. The American attitude deeply shocked the South Vietnamese that their ally would not keep their promise.

Ford continued nevertheless to probe Congress for an urgent delivery of military equipment. On 27 March, he dispatched the US Army Chief of Staff, General Frederick C. Weyand, to South Vietnam to assess the situation. He reported that "It is possible that with abundant resupply and a great deal of luck, the government of South Vietnam would survive". However, he remained very pessimistic if the North Vietnamese committed an additional three divisions, an army corps, that would definitely alter the military balance. A fact confirmed by both American and South Vietnamese intelligence. Colonel William E. Le Gro, the senior staff officer of the US Defence Attaché Office (DAO), reported that "the 320B Division is currently enroute to ARVN III Corps area and that two other divisions currently deployed in the South or from the reserve will also move to III Corps in the next one to three months". What Le Gro did not realise, muddled by weak intelligence data, was that the Communists were in the process of sending eight more divisions to Saigon, and they would arrive in two weeks, not in one to three months. The progress made by PAVN in logistics and transportation, allowing the quick displacements of entire army corps, was still not fully appreciated by the ARVN planners with tragic circumstances. Weyand suggested an urgent resupply program to reequip the battered ARVN units arriving from the abandoned northern provinces, including two infantry divisions, a three-brigade Marine division, three to four Ranger groups, four armoured squadrons and nine artillery battalions. All these units would be fully operational by the summer if equipment from US Army depots could be delivered as quickly as possible. Weyand estimated that if the ARVN could hold until the rainy season, there was a slim chance that a truncated and diminished South Vietnam would survive. Otherwise, and as a last desperate measure, he suggested the provisional reintroduction of the American strategic air support, the sending back of the B-52 bombers.

Off course, President Ford could not contemplate this last recommendation. The only aid was the sending of some batteries of 105mm howitzers, as well as a small number of M41 tanks and M113 APCs by air, part of a delayed delivery package already funded the preceding Fiscal Year. Instead, discreetly, Ford ordered the planning of the withdrawal of the last Americans still in South Vietnam. He also initiated Operation Baby Lift, on 3 April, the evacuation by air of Vietnamese orphans on humanitarian grounds. However, the start of the operation ended in disaster when the next day a USAF C-5 Galaxy crashed on take-off from Tan Son Nhut, killing 78 Vietnamese children and 50 adults. Meanwhile, in a top-secret operation, a USAF C-130 was sent to Dalat, in the southern Central Highlands area, with a team of technicians of the United States Atomic Energy Commission escorted by Navy SEALS, to retrieve the fuel rods from the nuclear research reactor at Dalat University,

hours before the North Vietnamese occupied the city, and flew them to Johnston Atoll.

On 10 April, for the last time President Ford requested that Congress provide urgent additional aid to South Vietnam: $722 million for the military and $250 million for economic aid. Congress declined to act on the President's request and expressed doubt that the aid could arrive in time to be useful, or in any case, enable South Vietnam to survive. That decision was made while throughout the front lines the South Vietnamese had pulled themselves together and fought back desperately.

Vung Tau became the focal regrouping point for the 40,000 troops arriving from the northern provinces. It was urgent to reconstitute and reequip them. The JGS was however slow in responding, so it was prodded into action by the American officers of the DAO. Colonel Edward Pelosky, Chief of the Army Division, DAO, took the lead in encouraging General Dong Van Khuyen, the Chief of the ARVN Logistic Command to draw up a plan. However, Khuyen had been unable to secure clear data of the exact needs from the JGS and his first proposal was not only incomplete but unworkable. The unreality of the plan was aggravated by the fact that it was predicated on the availability of supplemental appropriation funds, not available, and the significant absence of a clear, fully coordinated statement of priorities. On 29 March, a more workable joint DAO and Logistic Command plan was established, and finally implemented by the JGS on 5 April.

Taking profit in a lull of enemy operations in early April, the ARVN reorganised its units. On a tactical scale, what remained of the II Corps area, the last two coastal provinces of Binh Thuan and Ninh Thuan were incorporated into III Corps. At the forefront of the enemy advance was the port city of Phan Rang, on Route 1. The North Vietnamese missed a golden opportunity by not pushing down south along Route 1 after their 10th Division had taken Cam Ranh as there were few ARVN forces left to protect Phan Rang, apart from some RF/PF troops. Seeing the arrival of a mass of unruly refugees and deserters who began looting, the Ninh Thuan Province governor in Phan Rang fled. There remained only the local airbase with the attached 6th Air Division of VNAF Brigadier General Pham Ngoc Sang, whose pilots had been intensively involved in support of the fighting in the Central Highlands. The base was furthermore overcrowded when part of the 2nd Air Division that had evacuated Nha Trang AB temporarily sought asylum there. With a dwindling number of RF troops and VNAF guards to assure the security of its perimeter, the airbase could be overwhelmed at any time. By waiting, a mass of refugees flocked into it, hoping to be evacuated by air, disrupting the air operations. However, the situation improved when two C-130As of the RAAF sent by the Australian government to help evacuate refugees were used for the task. On 3 April, four US Navy ships were observed in the waters off Phan Rang. The cargo ship USS *Durham* was sent in to investigate and dozens of small boats loaded with refugees quickly surrounded her. Over the next two days, the *Durham* picked up almost 3,500 refugees. VNAF Lieutenant Colonel Le Van But flew his helicopter to meet the Americans, requesting that the destroyers escorting the *Durham* provide naval gunfire support. The Americans responded that they would only assist in refugee evacuations, not in providing direct support to their former ally.

One possible source of reinforcement were the 800 survivors of the 3rd Airborne Brigade of Lieutenant Colonel Le Van Phat, stranded around the M'Drak Pass on Route 21. After stemming the PAVN advance from Ban Me Thout for 12 days, the outnumbered unit broke out of their encircled positions and retreated into the

By the end of March 1975, President Ford sent US Army Chief of Staff, General Frederick C. Weyand, to South Vietnam to assess the situation. He is seen here, first on the left, during a meeting with US Ambassador Graham Martin, second from left, and President Nguyen Van Thieu. (VNN)

jungle and mostly regrouped on two hills. The VNAF 6th Air Division mounted a daring rescue operation on 3 April, mobilising 45 UH-1H transports, 12 UH-1H gunships and six CH-47As, covered by eight A-37Bs, that succeeded in retrieving them. The recovered troops were immediately redeployed for the defence of Phan Rang AB. Saigon also sent in the 2nd Airborne Brigade of Colonel Nguyen Thu Luong, with its 3rd Battalion also arriving the same day on C-119Gs and C-130As. The rest of the 2nd Airborne Brigade, including the 7th and 11th Battalions, an artillery battalion, and support and logistic units, flew in from Bien Hoa. The airlift was completed on 8 April, the C-130As bringing out the 3rd Airborne Brigade to Saigon for rest and reequipping.

In order to reinforce its northern flank, Lieutenant General Toan also ordered that the remaining element of the 2nd Division be evacuated by sea from Re Island and disembarked at Ham Tam to bolster the defences of Phan Rang. Its commander, Brigadier General Tran Van Nhut confronted a column of deserters rolling south down Route 1 towards the next coastal town of Phan Thiet. He ordered them to turn over their weapons and vehicles. In exchange they would be evacuated by sea towards Vung Tau. Those who refused would be shot. The VNN and requisitioned civilian ships moved in to evacuate them. Nhut picked up six M48 tanks of the 22nd Tank Squadron and 20 M113s of the 8th ACS, plus several artillery pieces and a large quantity of individual weapons. However, even if the 2nd Division was in the best shape of the three regular divisions from I Corps that had escaped the Da Nang enclave, that did not say much. Lieutenant General Toan transferred two RF battalions from III Corps to replace some of the division's losses, but Nhut could field only two understrength battalions per regiment. The JGS also sent reconnaissance teams from the elite Strategic Technical Directorate

The VNAF had the daunting task of reorganising its squadrons evacuated from the northern provinces into the three remaining main bases of Bien Hoa, Tan Son Nhut and Binh Thuy, with Phan Rang as an advanced operating base. This A-37B evacuated from Da Nang now operated from Bien Hoa. (VNAF)

Paradoxically, the disastrous course of events forced President Thieu to relinquish part of the prerogative the corps commanders had over VNAF units placed under their jurisdiction. The service regained in autonomy and markedly improved its efficiency during the last weeks of fighting of the war. An F-5A of the 542nd Fighter Squadron, 63rd Wing, of Bien Hoa is seen here waiting for another sortie. (Anthony Tambini)

to the northeast and northwest of Phan Rang to determine the current location of the Communist forces. They were inserted by helicopters, some of them disguised as North Vietnamese soldiers. Following Thieu's orders for no further retreats, Phan Rang would be held. Being the highest-ranking officer in place, VNAF Brigadier General Pham Ngoc Sang was designated the officer responsible for the defence of the city! Sang, fortunately for him, was soon replaced as the head of the Phan Rang front by Lieutenant General Nguyen Vinh Nghi, a former commander of the IV Corps who was volunteering for the task.

While provisionally stabilising the situation in front of Phan Rang, the JGS began a vast scheme for reconstituting units. As of 11 April, about 40,000 troops from I and II Corps had reported to training camps or had been reassigned to units in the III Corps area. The ARVN 2nd Division, which had been assembled at Ham Tan, had grown to 3,600, including two RF battalions assigned to it from Gia Dinh Province. The 3rd Division, on 11 April, had about 1,100 men at Ba Ria, Phuoc Tuy Province, and would be assigned another 1,000 soon, but it was short of all types of weapons and equipment. The 1st Division was also at Ba Ria but with only two officers and 40 men. Near Long Hai was the 23rd Division with about 1,000 men and 20 rifles. Although desertions were heavy, many deserters were rounded up, and the net inflow of men was greater than the losses. Another way to bolster strength was to fill out regular regiments with RF soldiers by disbanding RF groups. The process had already been implemented in IV Corps in the Mekong Delta area with great success. That process was principally directed towards the current units in the III Corps as well as the 22nd Division of II Corps, evacuated by sea from Qui Nhon. Rebuilt with only two regiments, some 4,600 men, the unit was redeployed without artillery along Route 4, south of Saigon on 12 April. The two depleted Marine brigades retrieved from Da Nang were also reconstituted into a diminished Marine Division and acted as a reserve for III Corps. Of the 12,000 Marines who had been deployed in the I Corps area, about 4,000 were at Vung Tau. Another serious problem was the shortage of Marine commanders: five battalion commanders, and 40 company commanders had been killed in action during March and April. The straggling Rangers regrouped at Vung Tau were filling the ranks of the current Ranger units.

In the command arena, on 3 April Lieutenant General Nguyen Van Minh, former commander of III Corps and now ARVN inspector general, was placed in command of the Capital Military District, replacing Admiral Chung Tan Cang. Cang was put back in charge of the Navy, replacing acting chief Admiral Lam Nguon Tanh.

President Thieu's decision to reinstall Cang, a staunch supporter, was not made to improve naval efficiency. It was to prevent Vice Air Marshal Nguyen Cao Ky from using the Navy to support a coup. Cang's first action as Navy commander was to create a new Riverine Task Force, TF-99, under Captain Le Huu Dong. Dong reported directly to Cang, and his task force was deliberately based at Nha Be, close to Saigon. TF-99 was formed from parts of two existing task forces in the Mekong Delta, TF-212 and TF-214. This decision also had political motivations. Ostensibly, TF-99 was to protect Saigon and the upper Mekong Rivers from increased enemy sapper interdiction. In reality, Cang had taken away the best units of two potential rival Navy officers that were reputedly close with Ky.

The VNAF also met immensurable problems while attempting to cope with the task of withdrawing units from long-established bases, or at least withdrawing its crucially important aircraft and personnel. Most of the aircraft arrived on their new bases in the south without ground support equipment, lacking spares and even the most basic tools. At least as important was the lack of personnel, notably mechanics and other specialists, many had been killed, captured, or abandoned in enemy territory. The evacuated airmen were therefore integrated into current units or were regrouped under the units that were the most intact and that had been able to escape.

Another incident that added to the VNAF problems was the bombing of the Presidential Palace on 8 April by Lieutenant Nguyen Thanh Trung of the 544th Fighter Squadron. Taking off from Bien Hoa AB and part of a flight of three F-5Es for a strike mission in the area of Phan Rang, Trung aborted after announcing a technical issue. He then dived low to avoid radar detection, before heading straight towards the palace. He dropped four 250lb bombs, with three exploding and damaging the building. President Thieu was at that time holding a meeting in a basement bomb shelter. Trung then recovered at the Song Be airfield north of Saigon, in North Vietnamese hands. Trung turned out to be a Communist agent and his infiltration into the VNAF was indeed a masterstroke by the PAVN intelligence.

Since 1973, the highly efficient centralised VNAF command organisation, having to use the available assets with utmost efficiency, had suffered a severe downgrading. The Air Force units were now placed directly under the command of each army corps commander for political reasons by President Thieu. Consequently, each of them had the tendency to use "his air force" only for his own needs and there was little coordination between Corps related to their respective aviation units. The quick firepower delivery and mobility that the Air Force allowed in response to an emergency situation on a national scale was then nullified. The series of catastrophic events had now forced Thieu to accept that the VNAF headquarters took back most of its assets for more efficient use. This system was based around a General Headquarters, the Tactical Air Control Centre

(TACC) at Tan Son Nhut AB that oversaw a series of regional headquarters, or Direct Air Support Centres (DASC), established at each ARVN Corps headquarters. Each DASC controlled the Air Liaison Officers (ALO) posted to various ARVN units, as well as the Forward Air Control (FAC) – Air Observation squadrons. Despite losing half of its DASCs, the remaining centres responded rather well to the urgency of the situation. During the last month of the war, the VNAF provided more coordinated air support to the Army, operating from its main remaining bases of Tan Son Nhut, Bien Hoa (III DASC), Binh Thuy (IV DASC), and the exposed airfield of Phan Rang. The TACC operated now along the following guidelines: around 100 tactical sorties for III Corps per day, 60 sorties for IV Corps, and 20 sorties reserved exclusively for use against targets of its own determination.

7

MARCHING SOUTH

With the rapid collapse of ARVN forces in the Da Nang and Central Highlands areas, the Politburo met again on 31 March to assess the situation. With Le Duan presiding, it concluded that strategically, militarily and politically, the Communists were holding the upper hand and the possibility of the enemy collapsing was high. In a fiery call to arms, Giap urged his Politburo colleagues to strike now, to not lose that great opportunity. He recommended quickly developing a battle plan to strategically surround Saigon from the east and the west, and use a powerful main force "fist" to make a surprise deep strike aimed at destroying the enemy. The formula for this strategy was "lightning speed, daring, surprise, certain victory".

The decision was unanimous, and the next day Le Duan sent new instructions to Pham Hung, Le Duc Tho and Van Tien Dung. Summarising Giap's briefing, he told them that after destroying some 35 percent of the ARVN, wiping out two army corps, liberating 12 provinces and increased the population of the liberated zones to nearly eight million, it was time to successfully end the war in the shortest time. The best way was to start that decisive battle and end it in April of this year, without any delay. The historic Politburo meeting approved three significant decisions: send the 1st, 2nd, and 3rd SACs to help conquer the South Vietnamese capital; use the B2

Symbolically the Provisional Revolutionary Government of South Vietnam, the political paravent of the Vietcong communist movement, moved to Hue, the ancient imperial capital by early April 1975. It organised a military parade in front of the main entrance of the Imperial Palace with PAVN troops of the 2nd SAC before it moved south. An SA-2 of the 274th SAM Regiment, 675th Anti-Aircraft Artillery Division, is seen here participating in the parade. (PAVN)

The 126th Naval Infantry Regiment also appeared on GAZ-63 trucks during the same military parade in Hue. The unit was held in reserve for amphibious operations behind ARVN lines. Finally, it was sent to capture the islands held by the South Vietnamese in the Spratly Archipelago. (PAVN)

Front forces to attack ARVN units in III Corps to see if they would immediately collapse; and conquer Saigon by the end of April 1975.

Giap sketched the basic North Vietnamese battle plan: strengthening the PAVN forces on the western approaches to Saigon, encircling and isolating the city from the southwest, and completely cut Route 4 to isolate Saigon from the Mekong Delta. The forces in the north and the east would attack and capture important targets and encircle and isolate Saigon from Ba Ria and Vung Tau, cutting any escape routes towards the sea. The motorised units would constitute powerful "deep penetration" groups with tanks and artillery that would be prepared to strike directly into the most critical enemy targets in the centre of Saigon when the opportunity presented itself.

If the North Vietnamese themselves were taken by surprise by the pace of the military developments since March 1975, Beijing, and Moscow, who were neither well informed of the situation in Vietnam nor had much control of developments there, were just astounded. Hanoi was approached by their allies for explanations while, in the meantime, Giap requested additional military aid to back up his final campaign. He particularly requested the urgent deliveries of additional tank and heavy artillery shells. In fact, the relationship with the Chinese continued to deteriorate, Beijing accusing the North Vietnamese of not seeking a political outcome to the conflict in favour of an "adventurist" military option. Already, in August and October 1974, the North Vietnamese requests for aid were turned down. The high profile given to the Khmer Rouge leader Khieu Sampahn's visit in April 1974 where he met Mao Zedong in contrast to the low-key publicity of North Vietnamese Prime Minister Pham Van Dong's visit in the same month added fuel to the already strained Sino-North Vietnamese relations.

Although details are still lacking, the North Vietnamese obtained better results with the Soviets. While they still had differences with the Russians, by continuing to refrain from taking sides in the Sino-

By early April 1975, the PAVN strategic reserve, the 1st SAC, was ordered to deploy south to assemble northeast of Saigon. The troops are seen here preparing the tanks of the constituent 202nd Armoured Brigade as well as the SA-2 missiles of the 367th Anti-Aircraft Artillery Division. (PAVN)

Soviet ideological dispute, and by continuing to procrastinate over joining the Soviet-led Council for Mutual Economic Assistance (COMECON), Hanoi had continued to deepen its relations with

Moscow since the end of the 1960s. The Soviet chief military adviser in North Vietnam, Lieutenant General Alexander Hyupenen, swiftly forwarded to Moscow Giap's requests. Part of them were fulfilled by an urgent aid program.

Moreover, the Politburo established a Council for the Support of the Battlefield, headed by Prime Minister Pham Van Dong in charge of coordinating all the ministries' efforts for forwarding men and equipment to the South. The entire North Vietnamese military transportation system, a total of 120,000 personnel, was mobilised for the task of forwarding troops and equipment. It was reinforced by mobilised civilian assets both in North and South Vietnam as necessary. Some 17,000 trucks, 32 oceangoing ships and 130 railroad trains were marshalled. The trains moved supplies into the southern part of North Vietnam where they were transferred into trucks. For the first time, the Navy transported by sea not only troops but also tanks and heavy artillery to the newly conquered ports of Quang Tri, Da Nang, Qui Nhon, or Cam Ranh Bay. Many ARVN prisoners and South Vietnamese civilians were pressganged to drive the captured trucks. Some 426 South Vietnamese civilian trucks and buses were also requisitioned.

A troop of folk dancers of the Propaganda Department entertained troops of the 202nd Armoured Brigade just before the unit received orders to move south for the final offensive against Saigon. (PAVN)

The whole North Vietnamese armoured corps was sent south to participate to the final offensive of the war. These SU-100 tank destroyers travelled part of the journey on railroad flat cars. At the South Vietnamese border, they would continue on their own tracks. (PAVN)

The main PAVN formations received their march orders, moving along three axes. The 2nd SAC, after securing Da Nang, would be heading along the coastal Route 1. The newly constituted 3rd SAC would move down the Central Highlands along Route 14. The 1st SAC would move from North Vietnam along both the Ho Chi Minh Trail's Main Corridor on the western side of the Annamite cordillera and the new Ho Chi Minh East, on its eastern side. On 1 April, the PAVN General Staff immediately shifted the 1st SAC, the strategic central reserve, towards the DMZ. Only its 308th Division, long considered the PAVN's most elite division, would remain behind to defend North Vietnam. The 1st SAC's ultimate destination was an assembly area at Dong Xoai in Phuoc Long province, some 95km northeast of Saigon. It was to arrive by 15 April.

Trains loaded with troops, weapons, and ammunition ran straight from the Hang Co Train Station in Hanoi to Vinh. From there trucks and ships carried the troops and supplies onward by land and sea. Despite the tremendous progresses in developing their logistic corridors, it still would be an enormous undertaking for the

North Vietnamese to shift an entire army corps over 1,200km along dirt roads and high mountain passes, across numerous streams and deep valleys. Giap made it clear that the troops had to be self-reliant and overcome most obstacles on their own, making repairs, fixing roads and bridges. An advanced corps element immediately departed on a convoy of 1,000 trucks until reaching Vinh where the 66th Armoured Battalion and some artillery pieces were transported by ships down to Quang Tri. For the first time in the war, North Vietnamese ships carried a complete armoured unit to the South. The rest of the column, followed by the 320B Division and the 367th Anti-Aircraft Artillery Division continued down the highway until reaching that last location. Closely following were the 312th Division, the 202nd Armoured Brigade, the 45th Artillery Brigade, and the assorted rear-service units. But despite Hanoi's constant urging of speed, the PAVN had only enough trucks to move one division at a time. Consequently, it had to implement truck shuttles, with the 320B Division moving first. For instance, when the division reached Dong Ha on 2 April, it switched to trucks belonging to

Troops of the 1st SAC loaded some ZIL-131 trucks with supplies for the long trek towards the South. (PAVN)

For the first time in the war, the North Vietnamese Navy carried complete armoured and artillery units to the South. These M-46 130mm long-range guns are seen being embarked at Haiphong Harbour. (PAVN)

Logistic Army 559 that was overseeing the Ho Chi Minh Trail, while the trucks it had been riding in returned north.

On 5 April, the 320B Division sped through southern Laos, behind it the 312th Division reached Dong Ha after a long trip on the same trucks that had ferried the 320B to the town. The corps headquarters then contacted Logistic Army 559 to switch vehicles again, and the trucks that had brought the 312th Division south returned to North Vietnam to pick up more troops. The 312th Division would continue south along the same route and on the same trucks used by the 320B. Despite the stretches of bad road and heavy traffic, by ferrying in this manner, the 1st SAC elements were able to move south fairly rapidly, the vehicles driving 18 to 20 hours per day. Each truck had two drivers and absolute priority would be given to them for rations and sleep.

Travelling in shifts, the advance corps element, mainly from the 320B Division, arrived in Dong Xoai on 11 April. By 14 April, all remaining corps units except the 202nd Armoured Brigade had also arrived, one day earlier than the General Staff's plan. The tanks were still struggling along Routes 9, 22 and 14, crossing six major rivers, accompanied by fuel cistern trucks. In fact, massing a maximum of tanks was the prerequisite for the final campaign of the war. As already indicated, the remaining armoured units kept in reserve were sent south. The 201st and 215th Armoured Brigades, with respectively four and three battalions, as well as the 206th Armoured Regiment, with two battalions, were ordered to leave by early April. They were followed by the 207th Armoured Regiment, a training unit. By using the armour kept in storage as well as the captured South Vietnamese tanks and APCs, some five new armoured battalions were also created. These units were partially staffed by the instructors of the Armour School. These were the 1B Battalion in the Central Highlands, the 775th Battalion in Nha Trang, the 675th

North Vietnamese troops were also moved in by ships, docking at the newly conquered Da Nang, Quy Nhon, Nha Trang, and Cam Ranh harbours. (PAVN)

A company of BTR-60 APCs of the PAVN 202nd Armoured Brigade, 1st SAC, en route along the Ho Chi Minh Trail. The unit reached its assembly area on 20 April. (PAVN)

battalion in Da Nang, and the 572nd Battalion in Hue. Even if their training was incomplete, it was hoped that they could be engaged in combat operation by the end of April.

Although other units continued to straggle in, the 1st SAC, the PAVN's most powerful combat unit, had accomplished an amazing feat, rapidly travelling nearly 2,000km in two short weeks and was now poised at the very gates of Saigon. It was joined by the 3rd

Practically two thirds of the massive North Vietnamese air defence system was redeployed south to protect the PAVN battle corps marching on Saigon. That included the S-125 (SA-3) Pechoras of the 277th SAM Regiment. (PAVN)

Concurrently with the deployment of the 1st SAC, the PAVN's newly constituted 3rd SAC in the Central Highlands was also redirected towards Saigon. Its advance was delayed by several air strikes carried out by the VNAF's Phan Rang-based 92nd Wing. This convoy of trucks was caught by an attack by A-37Bs along Local Route 450. (PAVN)

SAC coming down from the Central Highlands along Route 14 through Duc Lap and Dong Xoai with the 316th Division leading. It was accompanied by the 273rd Armoured Regiment, the 675th Artillery Regiment, as well as the 312th Anti-Aircraft Artillery Regiments. The corps was helped by the 471st Truck Division of Logistic Army 559 by ferrying the 320th Division that was still in the area of Thuy Hoa on the coast. However, it was the 10th Division that encountered the most difficulties. The division was still at Cam

Ranh when it was also ordered to turn around, and returned to the Central Highlands by using Local Route 450 up to Route 20. The 7th and 375th Engineer Regiments led the way, opening the road and building bridges. Thousands of Montagnard tribesmen were also requisitioned as porters and labourers. However, the movements of the 10th Division did not go unnoticed by VNAF O-1 FACs and EC-47 SIGINT aircraft. The three A-37B squadrons of the Phan Rang-based 92nd Wing of Colonel Le Van Thao, reinforced by a detachment of A-1 Skyraiders from Bien Hoa AB, were sent to attack the convoys. North Vietnamese sources reported that dozens of trucks were set ablaze but the drivers and engineers stoically pressed on, repaired the bomb damage, and continued building and repairing the road. On 15 April, most of the 3rd SAC reached Dau Tieng and occupied jumping-off positions for the attack on Saigon from the northwest in accordance with Giap's plan. Logistic Army 559 continued to bring in supplies for the new battlefield, and by mid-April 1975, the supply stockpiles had grown to 58,000 tons, including 24,000 tons of weapons and ammunition, 21,000 tons of rice, and 11,000 tons of POL. On 17 April, a special convoy of 240 trucks carrying 13,000 130mm artillery shells, 440 trucks carrying spare parts for the tanks, and 150 trucks carrying other ammunition and equipment left for the South.

The 2nd SAC took more time to reorganise. The Corps had only two thirds of the required trucks to move all of its units, so the General Headquarters sent in as reinforcement the 571st Truck Division of Logistic Army 559. Many units were still scattered far afield, particularly the artillery units deployed in firebases atop tall mountains. Some of them left their guns in place and took over the captured ARVN howitzers. The core of the 2nd SAC departed Da Nang and moved down Route 1 only on 7 April, with the 203rd Armoured Brigade leading. The 324th Division was left behind to protect Da Nang and Hue and to serve as a reserve force. Route 1 between Da Nang and Xuan Loc was a good, paved road for vehicular movement but there were 569 bridges and 588 culverts along the way, among which were 14 bridges across large rivers. Many of them had been blown up by the enemy. The General Staff sent the 83rd Bridge-Building Engineer Regiment to reinforce the Corps and also sent a number of oceangoing ships to transport troops from Da Nang to Quy Nhon.

From Phan Rang forward enemy forces were still quite numerous, deployed in strong defensive positions, so the Corps would adopt the attack on the march tactic. At the head of the "coastal column" was the first echelon with some 89 tanks and APCs, 223 artillery tractors, towing 87 guns and 136 anti-aircraft guns, as well as 2,276 trucks. Some 487 captured trucks and 100 requisitioned civilian

Despite persistent air attacks, the 7th and 375th Engineer Regiments of the 3rd SAC continued to improve the routes taken by the vehicles. This column of ZIL-130 trucks is seen crossing a pontoon bridge laid over the Sre Pok River. (PAVN)

By 15 April, the 3rd SAC finally reached the lowlands after crossing the southern part of the Annamite Cordillera for its assembly area at Dau Tieng, northwest of Saigon. These trucks crossing a makeshift bridge built by the engineer troops illustrate the variety of vehicles equipping the North Vietnamese Army. Leading is a GAZ-53 with a fuel cistern, followed by a Ural-375, and a ZIL-157. (PAVN)

Heading to the assembly area of the 3rd SAC is this Mazur 350 tracked artillery tractor towing a mobile command post on a trailer. (PAVN)

Departing from Da Nang for Saigon, the PAVN's 2nd SAC had to cross numerous rivers along the coastal Route 1 where many bridges had been destroyed by the retreating enemy. Despite being amphibious, these K-63 APCs crossed a river on a motorised barge under the protection of a Type 63 tank of the 203rd Armoured Brigade. (PAVN)

Further down Route 1, the vanguard first echelon of the 2nd SAC crossed another river on a pontoon bridge beside the destroyed original bridge. (APVN)

In some stretches Route 1 closely paralleled the coastline, giving occasion to the South Vietnamese Navy to carry out harassing shore bombardments. Apart from the ZIL-157 truck at the front, this column was mainly made up of captured M35 trucks as well as requisitioned civilian buses for transporting troops of the 2nd SAC. (PAVN)

This artillery unit of the 164th Artillery Brigade, 2nd SAC, also moved down Route 1. Leading was a captured M54 truck towing a D-74 122mm gun, followed an ATS-59 tracked tractor, and captured M35 trucks.

A battalion of SA-2s of the 274th SAM Regiment, 675th Anti-Aircraft Artillery Division, 2nd SAC is seen here heading towards Saigon on Route 1. (PAVN)

trucks followed, carrying 4,000 tons of weapons and ammunition that had been captured in the Hue and Da Nang areas. The political commissars constantly exhorted the men to press forward, recalling the "historic task" bestowed on them to reunify the country. Giap's motto "speed and daring" was painted on the vehicles, on the helmets, on the trees lining the route. With many vehicles having two drivers, rolling days and nights, bypassing destroyed bridges or crossing rivers on pontoon bridges laid down by the engineers, the advance was fairly fast, driving through areas already fallen into the hands of the Communists. There was even a leg of 185km completed in one day. The leading elements reached Cam Ranh Bay on 11 April where it was reinforced with an additional 40 tanks brought in there by the North Vietnamese Navy.

BIBLIOGRAPHY

Anon, *Lich Su Binh Chung Thiet Giap Quan Doi Nhan Dan Viet Nam 1959 – 1975 – PAVN Armour Corps History 1959–1975* (Ha Noi: Nha Xuat Ban Quan Doi Nhan Dan, 1982)

Anon, *Lich Su Bo Doi Truong Son Duong Ho Chi Minh* – Troops of the Ho Chi Minh Trails History (Ha Noi: NhaXuat Ban Quan Doi Nhan Dan, 1994)

Anon, *Lich Su Cong Binh Viet Nam 1945 – 1975 – PAVN Engineer Corps History 1945–1975* (Ha Noi, Nha Xuat Ban Quan Doi Nhan Dan, 1991)

Anon, *Lich Su Hai Quan Nhan Dan Viet Nam – PAVN Navy History* (Ha Noi: Nha Xuat Ban Quan Doi Nhan Dan, 1985)

Anon, *Lich Su Lu Doan Tang 202 – PAVN 202nd Armoured Brigade History* (Ha Noi: Nha Xuat Ban Quan Doi Nhan Dan, 1984)

Anon, *Lich Su Lu Doan Tang 203 – PAVN 203rd Armoured Brigade History* (Ha Noi: Quan Doan 2 Xuat Ban, 1990)

Anon, *Lich Su Phao Binh Quand Doi Nhan Dan Viet Nam, Tap 2 – PAVN Artillery Branch History Volume 2* (Ha Noi: Nha Xuat Ban Quan Doi Nhan Dan, 1986)

Anon, *Lich Su Quan Chung Phong Khong – PAVN Air Defence Command History*, 2 vols (Hanoi: Nha Xuat Ban Quan Doi Nhan 1991 and 1993)

Anon, *Su Doan 303 – PAVN 303rd Division History* (Hanoi : Nha Xuat Ban Quan Doi Nhan Dan, 1989)

Anon, *Su Doan 7 – PAVN 7th Division History* (Hanoi : Nha Xuat Ban Quan Doi Nhan Dan 1990)

Anon, *Su Doan Quan Tien Phong, Su Doan 308 – PAVN 308th Division History* (Hanoi : Nha Xuat Ban Quan Doi Nhan Dan, 1979)

Anon, *Su doan Sao Vang: Binh Doan Chi Lang Quan khu 1 – PAVN Gold Star Division: Chi Lang Corps, Military Region 1* (Hanoi: NXB Quan Doi Nhan Dan, 1984)

Anon, *The Ho Chi Minh Campaign, Memoirs of War: Reminiscences of Revolutionary Commanders and Political Commissars* (Hanoi: The Gioi Publishers, 2012)

Anon, *Tu Dien Bach Khoa Quan Su Viet Nam – Vietnamese Military Dictionary* (Hanoi: Bo Quoc Phong Nha Xuat Ban Quan Doi Nhan Dan, 1996)

Anon, *Ve Dai Thang Mui Xuan Nam 1975 Quoc Tai Lieu Cua Chinh Quyen Sai Gon – The 1975 Great Spring Victory through Saigon Government Documents* (Hanoi: Nha Xuat Ban Quoc Gia Trinh Tri, 2010)

Boivineau, G., *La Force introuvable, Vietnam 1965-1975* (Paris: Les Indes Savantes, 2021)

Bowers, R. L., *Tactical Airlift* (Washington: Office of Air Force History & GPO, 1983)

Brigham, R. K., *ARVN: Life and Death in the South Vietnamese Army* (Lawrence: University Press of Kansas, 2006)

Brisay, Captain T. D., *Fourteen Hours at Koh Tang* (Washington: USAF Southeast Asia Monograph Series, Volume III, Monographs 4 and 5, GPO, 1977)

Cao Ky, N., *Budha's Child: My fight to save Vietnam* (New York: St Martin's Press, 2002)

Collins, Brig. Gen. J. L., *The Development and Training of the South Vietnamese Army, 1950-1972* (Washington: Department of the Army, 1986)

Conboy, K., Bowra, K., *The NVA and Viet Cong* (Oxford: Osprey Publishing, 1991)

Currey, C. B., *Victory at Any Cost: The Genius of Vietnam's Gen. Vo Nguyen Giap* (Washington: Brasse's Inc., 1997)

Darcour, P., *Vietnam, qu'as-tu fait de tes fils?* (Paris: Editions Albatros, 1975)

Des Brisay, Capt. Thomas D., *USAF Southeast Asia Monograph Series, Volume III, Monograph 5: Fourteen Hours at Koh Tang* (Washington: GPO, 1977)

Dorr, R. F., *Air War South Vietnam* (London: Arms and Armour Press, 1990)

Duc Phuong, N., *Chien Thanh Viet Nam, Toan Tap. Tu Tran Dau (Ap Bac – 1963) den Tran Cuoi (Saigon – 1975) – The Vietnam War, from the first (Ap Bac 1963) to the last (Saigon 1975) battles* (Toronto: Lang Van Publishers, 2001)

Duiker, William, J., *Sacred War: Nationalism and Revolution in a Divided Vietnam* (New York: McGraw-Hill, 1995)

Gaiduk, I. V., *The Soviet Union and the Vietnam War* (Chicago: Ivan R Dee, 1996)

Giap, V. N., *Tong Hanh Dinh Trong Mua Xuan Toan Thang – At the General Headquarters during the victorious Spring* (Hanoi: Nha Xuat Ban Chinh Tri Quoc Gia., 2000)

Gilbert, M. J., *Why the North Won the Vietnam War* (New York: Palgrave, 2002)

Grandolini Albert, *Target Saigon, Volume 2: The Fall of South Vietnam: The Beginning of the End, January 1974–March 1975* (Warwick: Helion and Company,, 2020).

Grandolini, A., *Armor of the Vietnam War; Asian Forces* (Hong Kong: Concord Publications Company, 1998)

Grandolini, A., *Fall of the Flying Dragon: South Vietnamese Air Force 1973-1975* (Houston: Harpia Publishing, 2011)

Grandolini, A., *Target Saigon, Volume 1: The Pretence of Peace* (Solihull: Helion and Company,, 2017)

Grandolini, A., *The Easter Offensive, Volume 1: Invasion Across the DMZ* (Solihull: Helion and Company,, 2015)

Grandolini, A., *The Easter Offensive, Volume 2: Tanks in the Streets* (Solihull: Helion and Company,. 2015)

Guan, A. C., *Ending the Vietnam War* (New York: Routledge Curzon, 2009)

Guan, A. C., *The Vietnam War from the Other Side: The Vietnamese Communists' Perspective* (London and New York: Routledge Curzon Taylor & Francis, 2002)

Hinh, Major-General N. D. & Tho, Brigadier-General T. D., *Indochina Monographs: The South Vietnamese Society* (Washington: GPO 1980)

Hinh, Major-General N. D., *Indochina Monographs: Vietnamization and the Cease-Fire* (Washington: GPO, 1980)

Hosmer, S. T., Kellen, K., Jenkins, B. M. *The fall of South Vietnam: statements by Vietnamese military and civilian leaders* (New York City: Crane, Russak, 1980)

Isaacs, A. R., *Without Honor: Defeat in Vietnam and Cambodia* (Baltimore, Maryland: Johns Hopkins University Press, 1983)

Khuyen, Lieutenant-General, D. V., *Indochina Monographs: RVNAF Logistics* (Washington: GPO 1980)

Kim Do, Captain & Kane, J., *Counterpart: A South Vietnamese Naval Officer's War* (Annapolis: Naval Institute Press, 1998)

Kissinger, H., *Ending the Vietnam War: A History of America's Involvement in and Extraction from the Vietnam War* (New York: Simone & Schuster, 2003)

Le Gro, William E., *Indochina Monographs: Vietnam from Cease-Fire to Capitulation* (Washington: GPO, 1985)

Le Gro, William E., *Vietnam Combat Operations 1972 – 1975* (Newton, Connecticut, Defense Lion Publications, 2013)

Lien-Hang, T. N., *Hanoi's War: An International History of the War for Peace in Vietnam* (Chapel Hill: University of North Carolina Press, 2012)

Manh Dan, N. & Ngoc Hanh, N., *Vietnam in flames* (Saigon: The General Staff of the Armed Forces of the Republic of Vietnam, 1971)

Melson, C. D., and Arnold, C. G., *U.S. Marines in Vietnam: The War that Would Not end, 1971–1973* (Washington: History and Museums Division, 1991)

Mesko, J., *VNAF: South Vietnamese Air Force: 1945-1975* (Carrollton TX: Squadron/Signal Publications, 1987)

Mikesh, R. C., *Flying Dragons: The South Vietnamese Air Force* (Minneapolis: MBI Publishing, 1988)

Military History Institute of Vietnam (Translated by Merle L. Pribbenow), *Victory in Vietnam: The Official History of the People's Army of Vietnam 1954–1975* (Laurence: University of Kansas Press, 2002)

Momyer, General W. W., *USAF Southeast Asia Monograph Series, Volume III, Monograph 4: The Vietnamese Air Force, 1951–1975, an Analysis of its Role in Combat* (Washington: GPO, 1977)

Nalty, B. C., *Air War over South Vietnam, 1968–1975* (Washington: Air Force History and Museums Program, 2001)

Oliver, T., *Cruel April: The Fall of Saigon* (New York: Norton & Company, 1987)

Phong Dinh, P., *Chien Su Quan Luc Viet Nam Cong Hoa – One chapter for each division, and each other major component of the RVNAF, in the 1970s* (Winnipeg: Tu Sach Vinh Danh, 2001)

Prados, J., *Vietnam: The History of an Unwinnable War, 1945–1975* (Lawrence: University Press of Kansas, 2009)

Qiang, Z., *China and the Vietnam Wars, 1950–1975* (Chapel Hill, NC: The University of North Carolina Press, 2000)

Rottman, G. L., Bujeiro, R., *Army of the Republic of Vietnam 1955–75* (Oxford: Osprey Publishing Ltd, 2010)

Rottman, G. L., Volstad, R., *Vietnam Airborne* (Oxford: Osprey Publishing Ltd, 2012)

Snepp, F., *Decent Interval: An Insider's Account of Saigon's Indecent End, Told by CIA's Chief Strategy Analyst in Vietnam* (New York: Random House, 1977)

Starry, General D. A., *Mounted Combat in Vietnam* (Washington: US Army Centre of Military History, 1977)

Thai, H. V., *How South Vietnam was liberated* (Hanoi: The Gioi Publishers, 1992)

Thao, Major-General H. M., *The Victorious Tay Nguyen Campaign* (Hanoi: Foreign Language Publishing House, 1979)

Thao, Major-Gneeral H. M., *Memoirs of War: Military Operations in the Central Highlands* (Hanoi: The Gio Publishers, 2012)

Thi, L. Q., *The Twenty-Five Year Century: A South Vietnamese General Remembers the Indochina War to the Fall of Saigon* (Denton: University of North Texas Press, 2001)

Tho, Brig. Gen. T. D., *Indochina Monographs: Pacification* (Washington: GPO, 1980)

Tien Hung, N. & Schecter, J. L., *The Palace File* (New York City: Harper & Row, 1986)

Tin, B., *Following Ho Chi Minh: Memoirs of a North Vietnamese Colonel* (London: Christopher Hurst, 1995)

Tin, B., *From Friend to Enemy: A North Vietnamese perspective on the war* (Annapolis: Naval Institute Press, 2002)

Trieu, L. H., *Su Doan 10: Binh Doan Tay Nguyen (PAVN 10th Division History)* (Hanoi: Nha xuat ban Quan Doi Nhan Dan, 1987)

Truong, Lieutenant-General, N. Q., *Indochina Monographs: RVNAF and US Operational Cooperation and Coordination* (Washington: GPO, 1980)

Truong, Lieutenant-General, N. Q., *Indochina Monographs: Territorial Forces* (Washington: GPO, 1980)

Tue, D., Xuan, P. B., *1975: The artillery corps during the spring 1975 Offensive* (Hanoi: Nha xuat ban Quan Doi Nhan Dan, 1985)

Van Tra, T., *Nhung chang duong lich su cu B2 thanh dong, Vol. 5, Ket thuc cuoc chien tranh 30 nam, was* (Ho Chi Minh City: Van Nghe, 1982) (Translated as *Vietnam: History of the Bulwark B2 Theatre, vol. 5: Concluding the 30-Years War* (Springfield VA: NTIS, 1983)

Veith, G. J., *Black April, the fall of South Vietnam 1973–1975* (New York: Encounter Books, 2012)

Vien, General C.V., and Khuyen, Lieutenant-General D.V., *Indochina Monographs: Reflections on the Vietnam War* (Washington: GPO, 1980)

Vien, General C.V., *Indochina Monographs: Leadership* (Washington: GPO, 1980)

Vien, General C.V., *Indochina Monographs: The Final Collapse* (Washington: GPO, 1983)

Viet, H. M., *Steel and Blood; South Vietnamese Armor and the War for Southeast Asia* (Annapolis: Naval Institute Press, 2008)

Vinh Le, T., *Vietnam où est la vérité?* (Paris: Lavauzelle, 1989)

Wiest, A., *Vietnam's Forgotten Army: Heroism and Betrayal in the ARVN* (New York: NYU Press, 2008)

Willbanks, J. H., *Abandoning Vietnam: How America Left and South Vietnam Lost Its War* (Lawrence, Kansas: University of Kansas Press, 2004)

Williams, B., *The Kissinger Transcripts: The Top Secret Talks with Beijing and Moscow* (New York: The New Press, 1998)

Xuan, D. T. M., *1975: Victorious Spring of 1975* (Hanoi: Nha xuat ban Quan Doi Nhan Dan, 2005)

Xuang Dung, T., *Chien Su Thuy Quan Luc Chien, Quan Luc Viet Nam Cong Hoa – History of the Vietnamese Marine Corps, Army of the Republic of Vietnam* (Toronto: Tran Xuan Dung ed., 1997)

About the Author

Albert Grandolini

Military historian and aviation-journalist Albert Grandolini was born in Vietnam and gained an MA in history from Paris 1 Sorbonne University. His primary research focus is on contemporary conflicts in general and particularly on the military history of Asia and Africa. Having spent his childhood in South Vietnam, the Vietnam War has always been one of his main fields of research. He authored the book *Fall of the Flying Dragon: South Vietnamese Air Force (1973-1975)*, two volumes on the Vietnam Easter Offensive of 1972 for Helion's Asia@War Series, and three volumes on Libyan Air Wars for the Africa@War Series. This is his third volume of *Target Saigon* for the Asia@War series. He has also written numerous articles for various British, French, and German magazines.